GOOD TO GO

GOOD TO GO

A Fresh Take on Potty Training for Today's Intentional Parent

GIA GAMBARO BLOUNT
LAURA BIREK

BLOOMSBURY ACADEMIC
NEW YORK • LONDON • OXFORD • NEW DELHI • SYDNEY

BLOOMSBURY ACADEMIC

Bloomsbury Publishing Inc, 1385 Broadway, New York, NY 10018, USA
Bloomsbury Publishing Plc, 50 Bedford Square, London, WC1B 3DP, UK
Bloomsbury Publishing Ireland, 29 Earlsfort Terrace, Dublin 2, D02 AY28, Ireland

BLOOMSBURY, BLOOMSBURY ACADEMIC and the Diana logo are trademarks of Bloomsbury Publishing Plc

First published in the United States of America 2025

Copyright © Gia Gambaro Blount and Laura Birek, 2025

Cover image: © istock/baona

All rights reserved. No part of this publication may be: i) reproduced or transmitted in any form, electronic or mechanical, including photocopying, recording or by means of any information storage or retrieval system without prior permission in writing from the publishers; or ii) used or reproduced in any way for the training, development or operation of artificial intelligence (AI) technologies, including generative AI technologies. The rights holders expressly reserve this publication from the text and data mining exception as per Article 4(3) of the Digital Single Market Directive (EU) 2019/790.

Bloomsbury Publishing Inc does not have any control over, or responsibility for, any third-party websites referred to or in this book. All internet addresses given in this book were correct at the time of going to press. The author and publisher regret any inconvenience caused if addresses have changed or sites have ceased to exist, but can accept no responsibility for any such changes.

A catalog record for this book is available from the Library of Congress

ISBN: HB: 979-8-76514-884-6
ePDF: 979-8-76514-886-0
eBook: 979-8-76514-885-3

Typeset by Deanta Global Publishing Services, Chennai, India
Printed and bound in the United States of America

For product safety related questions contact productsafety@bloomsbury.com.

To find out more about our authors and books visit www.bloomsbury.com and sign up for our newsletters.

To all the parents over the years who have trusted us to be part of their parenting journeys and have asked for this book—here you go!

CONTENTS

Introduction 1

PART I The *Good to Go* Method 5

1 Before We Start 7
2 The Big Picture: Essential Parenting Tools 13
3 Rethinking Readiness 35
4 Are YOU Ready? 49

PART II Ready, Set, Go 61

5 Ready to Start 63
6 Set the Stage 87
7 It's Go Time 119
8 Keep Going 141
9 Expect the Unexpected 161
10 Now We're Cruising 187

Conclusion 197

Resources 201
Acknowledgments 202
Index 205
About the Authors 209

Introduction

Why Should I Trust You, Anyway?

I'm a failure at potty training.

That's an interesting way to start a book about potty training, you're probably thinking. But it's true. The first time my child went diaper free, it was an unmitigated disaster.

My son, Auggie, was only twenty months old at the time. But I had been given a popular potty-training book that insisted he was READY. All I had to do was strip him naked, stay home for three days, have a lot of carpet cleaner ready, and we'd magically be done with diapers.

Everyone told me that this was the One True Way to achieve diaper freedom, and as a first-time mom, I had nothing to compare it to. I was in the second trimester with another son, Sebastian, and was eager to have Auggie potty trained before I was back in the postpartum fog.

For me, there was also a bit of a carpe diem attitude to it all. Here in California, wildfires were raging, turning the skies an apocalyptic dark orange and trapping us indoors for days on end. The world was burning down, I might as well try potty training! What did I have to lose?

A lot, it turns out.

While Auggie truly enjoyed being bare-butted for a long weekend, the transition back into clothes and the subsequent reintegration into normal life was rough. Sure, he was peeing and pooping in the potty (mostly), but not without constant vigilance on our parts. My husband and I had become potty task masters, turning into complete nags in an attempt to "remind" Auggie to use the facilities at regular intervals. There was a palpable undercurrent of stress about accidents any time we had to leave the house. It was no way to live.

Then Sebastian was born, and everything unraveled. Auggie started regressing and having pee accidents almost daily. We were all frustrated, as the potty-training book I read said we shouldn't give up in the face of these challenges. The book encouraged us to double down on the training and said that if we put Auggie back in diapers he'd internalize this as a personal failure.

It was at that time that I coincidentally ran into Gia. I had bundled up tiny newborn Sebastian to take him to a feeding support group at The Family Room, a local space that supports new parents with classes and community gatherings. When I arrived, I found Gia setting up for one of her toddler classes. Auggie and I had taken Gia's classes together, and she was eager to catch up with me (and hold my new baby).

I started telling Gia about Auggie's potty struggles, and I could tell she had nothing but sympathy . . . and brewing ideas. I call Gia "the toddler whisperer" for a reason: she is a genius when it comes to child behavior. And when she gets a good idea for a strategy, you can see it in her eyes. So, while I was venting about all the pee I was cleaning up off the floor, Gia's eyes were twinkling with inspiration.

Gia interrupted my ramblings to ask, "Laura, did Auggie even know potty training was about to happen, or did you just spring this on him?"

I was speechless. The book I had consulted had specifically warned me against doing any potty-training prep ahead of time, as it would "confuse" Auggie's little toddler brain. But hearing Gia say this, I realized I had basically blindsided Auggie with a huge life change, and just assumed he'd be okay with it.

Despite being dedicated to a respectful parenting style, where I was determined to treat Auggie as a full human deserving of the same emotional considerations as anyone else, I had failed to consider his feelings in this process. In all other aspects of parenting, I was gentle, patient, and collaborative. But when it came to ditching diapers, I was authoritarian, punitive, and impatient. Why had I treated potty training so differently?

I hurried back home and sat down in front of Auggie, looked him in the eyes, and told him I was sorry for all the pressure we put on him to use the potty. I then asked him if he wanted to wear diapers again. He instantly said "YES!" and we all felt a huge sense of relief as we paused potty training until we could find a better approach.

But was there actually a better way? Or were we just kicking the can down the road, doomed to repeat the same high-pressure and stressful process a few months later?

This question was at the front of my mind as Auggie approached his third birthday and was still in diapers. I had learned my lesson about pushing too hard, but I wasn't sure what the alternative was. Some of my favorite parenting resources had long blog posts about potty learning that could be simmered down to "they'll figure it out on their own." But I knew my son, and I knew Auggie was never going to spontaneously take it upon himself to go diaper free. There must be a middle ground between three-day potty training and the wait-and-see approach, I thought. But I couldn't find it.

Luckily, I still had Gia's number.

This book is the result of the conversations I've had with Gia about potty learning since then. Of course, Gia was abuzz with her own brilliant ideas about the topic. As a parenting educator with twenty years of experience working directly with toddlers, she had collected hundreds of stories from real parents attempting to go diaper free. And as the mother of two boys with wildly different personalities, she knows first hand how there's no one-size-fits-all approach.

With Gia's strategic yet intuitive approach, Auggie was able to transition to undies without drama just before he turned three.

Good to Go is here to bridge the gap between the two extreme ends of the current potty-training climate. We've compiled Gia's expertise and experience into a simple and easy-to-follow method that will help teach toilet independence without stress, pressure, or shame.

And I'll be along for the ride! As I type this, Sebastian is twenty-eight months old and, with Gia's help, we're going to attempt to go diaper free. Throughout the book I'll be reporting on his progress and any hiccups (or funny anecdotes) we encounter along the way.

A quick note about the format: while I'm the host of *Big Fat Positive*, a pregnancy and parenting podcast, and I love talking about myself, I'm going to let Gia take the reins for the rest of the book. I'll be showing up in sidebars, but otherwise please assume it's our parenting sage Gia who's speaking. Trust me, you need her wisdom in your life more than you need my silly pee jokes. Seriously, *urine good hands* . . .

—Laura Birek

PART I

THE *GOOD TO GO* METHOD

1

Before We Start

Potty Training Isn't Rocket Science. Apparently, It's Harder

"*Why is this so hard?*" This is a question I hear almost daily. Whether it's toddler tantrums or picky eating, first-time parents often come to me completely shocked at the curve balls their tiny humans throw at them. For over twenty years, I've taught parenting classes in Pasadena, right around the corner from CalTech and the Jet Propulsion Laboratory, where countless NASA engineers have come to me for help with potty training their toddlers. They've designed satellites and Mars rovers, but can't get their kid to poop in a toilet.

And that's okay! Children don't come with a manual, and all parents start at square one. Even with my master's in early childhood education, when I had my two boys, I realized no amount of schooling could have prepared me for the realities of parenthood. But now, with over two decades of professional and personal experience under my belt, I'm here to help. Parenting is always going to be surprising, but I'm here to make it easier for you and your child.

So who am I, and how can I pull off this magic trick? Well, I've read all the studies and books, taught in-person parenting classes for decades, and have talked with thousands of parents about their struggles. I don't ascribe to one particular parenting philosophy, but instead base my recommendations on the most up-to-date research combined with my experience and intuition.

I'm also a mother myself. My two boys couldn't be more different from one another, and those differences have given me the humble insight that there is no one, right way to parent.

Why This Book?

While I've guided thousands of families through their parenting journeys and have answered all kinds of questions lobbed at me from harried parents, one question has always stumped me: "What book do you recommend for potty training?"

Unfortunately, I never could, in good conscience, recommend anything that was on the market. I know potty training is a major stress point for parents, so I searched high and low for a good manual for my students. But the most popular books and video courses I found never quite hit the mark.

Existing resources seem to fall into two camps: the quick-fix method and the "wait and see" approach.

In my experience, books pushing early and rapid potty independence are overpromising and under-delivering. As a result, many parents experience major frustration with the process and often inadvertently create shame or fear surrounding using the toilet. In the worst case, these quick-fix books can cause lasting constipation and withholding problems, requiring ongoing help from pediatric urologists.

On the other hand, many gentle parenting experts may suggest avoiding any type of toilet learning and allowing your child to naturally ditch diapers "when they're ready." While this approach may work well for some families, it's unrealistic for many. Preschools will often require potty training before a child can enroll, forcing parents to train before the school year starts. Other kids have no internal motivation to use the toilet and feel perfectly fine using diapers for what seems like eternity.

My approach to toilet learning is somewhere in the middle. I strongly believe in honoring your child's bodily autonomy while providing structured guidance and support. I began teaching a unique potty-training method in my toddler classes, as well as in online toilet-independence workshops I developed. After these sessions, there were always follow-up questions, and I learned so much about the different challenges parents experienced with their unique and wonderful children. Over time, this process helped me develop and refine the *Good to Go* method.

During this time, Laura was taking a weekly Toddler & Me class at The Family Room. I had known Laura for almost four years by this point. Because she co-hosted a popular pregnancy and parenting podcast, *Big Fat Positive*, and was a bit of an expert herself, I would often bounce ideas off her before or after class.

I knew Laura hadn't been shy about sharing her disappointment with one of the most popular potty-training books out there, and how it failed with her first son, Auggie. So I asked her what she thought about turning my workshop into a book. She jumped right on board, and we got started writing *Good to Go*.

How Is *Good to Go* Different?

In *Good to Go*, we aim to provide an alternative to the polarizing models out there. We're not going to force potty independence over a long weekend, nor are we waiting until your kid decides to do it on their own.

Our approach is different. First, we teach caregivers some essential parenting concepts and tools. Then, we spend a few weeks in something we call "the rehearsal period," where your child practices the skills needed for independent pottying while they're still in diapers. Finally, we teach you exactly how to take away diapers and how to manage any challenges that come your way.

Part I goes over the theory and background you'll need to know before officially starting. This is where you'll find all the big-picture theories and fundamental parenting tools that will support you through potty training and beyond. Here, you will also find help in determining if and when it's time to start—both for your child and for you!

Part II covers the actual sequence, step by step. It gives detailed support for each stage of the process. First we'll go over prep: the gear you'll need, how to model and teach, and how to best prepare for success. Then we'll get into all the nitty-gritty details of how exactly to remove diapers. In this part, you'll find practical and actionable steps to achieve potty-training success.

While the main text of this book is in my voice and Laura's narrative shows up in sidebars, writing *Good to Go* has been a collaborative effort, shared equally between both authors. Laura and I have worked together to hone and refine the *Good to Go* method, and our combined expertise and experience are what make this book so special.

A Quick Note about Language

In writing this book, I'm taking care to use inclusive and respectful language. I will be using the gender-neutral pronouns they/them when referring to hypothetical parents or children, while I'll use a person's preferred pronouns when relating stories from my students.

Because this is a potty-training book, there will naturally be some discussion of genitals. I also recognize that there are parents of intersex children who will read this book and that those caregivers may need to adjust some of the advice to align with their child's anatomy. While I aim to be inclusive, it can be awkward to form a sentence around "child with a penis" or "child with a vulva," so I may revert to the shorthand of "boy" or "girl" occasionally. Please understand this is not meant to be exclusionary or erasing, but done for clarity and succinctness.

When I refer to "parents," I mean this as anyone engaging in the act of parenting. I fully recognize that families come in all forms and caregivers reading this book may not be biological or even adoptive parents. If you're a foster parent, grandparent, or anyone who has been entrusted with the care of a child, I hope you also feel seen and supported by this book. Similarly, I won't assume every family has two primary caregivers, or that every parent has a partner of a different gender.

When discussing bodily functions, I'll be calling urine "pee" or "#1," and bowel movements will be "poop" or "#2." This is just my personal choice, but you can call these things whatever your family likes or culture teaches. The only important thing is using consistent vocabulary during the process (we'll talk more about this in Part II).

Finally, I want to address the use of the term "potty training." As an educator, I don't love this phrase. "Training" is often associated with animal behavior, is something done to a child (as opposed to *with* a child), and doesn't account for your child's interests, preferences, or input.

"Toilet learning" and "potty independence" are more respectful and accurate, but, honestly, they're a little clunky. That's why I love the phrase "Good to Go" because it's positive and individualized. But, to reference the process, for lack of a better term, and to utilize the most recognizable and commonly used phrase, I'll still be using "potty training" throughout this book.

Whenever Laura talks about her children publicly, whether it's in her podcast or this book, she uses pseudonyms. ("Auggie" and "Sebastian" were the runner-up choices for their real names, which is how she picked them as pseudonyms!) I will also use aliases and obscure identifying details when discussing my own students, sometimes combining stories from multiple families to protect their privacy.

Finally, while I have a master's degree in early childhood education and twenty years of experience, I am not a doctor. I have made every attempt to provide information that is accurate and complete, but this book is not intended as a substitute for professional medical advice. This book is not meant to be used, nor should it be used, to diagnose or treat any medical or psychological condition. Please consult your own medical advisors whose responsibility it is to determine the condition of, and best treatment for, your child.

A Little Background

How and when we teach our children to use the potty has historical and cultural context. If you're reading this book, you likely have access to disposable diapers and weekly municipal trash service. Now, imagine a parent living in a rural area with no running water, electricity, or stores nearby. You could both have children the same age, with the same developmental skills, but the rural parent is going to have an incentive to potty train at a much earlier age.

It's important to acknowledge these contexts when we discuss choices around potty training. And it's not just about access: your culture may have different norms about when and how children learn to use the toilet. I never want to make light of or be dismissive of these cultural values; if you find anything in *Good to Go* that doesn't sit right, trust your gut and adjust accordingly. As you'll learn shortly, the core of my Values-Centered Parenting tool is to center your values above all else.

But if you're like most of my students, you probably live in a city or suburb and have access to disposable diapers at every corner store. It's a convenience most of us never think twice about, but the history is pretty interesting!

You may be surprised to learn how recently disposable diapers came on the scene. While the first one was invented in 1961, they didn't become widely available and affordable until the late 1970s. Before then, most American parents used cloth diapers, which necessitated a lot of laundry.

As a result, the average age of potty training in America in the 1950s was twelve months. Those exhausted parents must have had a lot of incentive to get those kids out of diapers. As disposable diapers trickled onto the market, that average age crept up to eighteen months. Nowadays, that number is somewhere around thirty months.

Without the historical context, one would look at these numbers and think that, somehow, babies were just different in the 1950s. But nothing has drastically changed about how babies and toddlers hit developmental milestones. What has changed is how and when caregivers start potty training, and how much they're involved long term. Those young toddlers in the 1950s likely needed the same amount of assistance in toileting that a similarly aged kid would need today.

"Great," you may be thinking. "But how do I know if my 21st-century toddler is ready to start?" Let's ditch the history lesson and get right into it!

2

The Big Picture
Essential Parenting Tools

Before we dive into the plan, let's go over some essential tools that are complete game changers when it comes to potty training and beyond. My superpower is taking existing child development theories and combining them with my own expertise to create new approaches to parenting. In this chapter, you'll find a distillation of what I teach my own students. What follows are some of the most effective and most loved tools that I've developed over the past twenty years.

When we first go over these tools, we'll discuss them in scenarios not related to potty training. By doing so, I'm hoping you'll gain a deeper understanding of how you can use these techniques in your everyday life and get some practice before potty training begins. Then, in later chapters, we'll revisit these fundamental tools in the context of potty training, so you can see exactly how to apply them in those situations.

You Teach, They Learn

At the start of this chapter all about big ideas in parenting, I want to first talk about the difference between teaching and learning. You can control how you approach the teaching. What you can't control is how your child learns.

Often, we think teaching and learning are one and the same: an instructor bestowing knowledge to a pupil, who absorbs it instantly. But we all know this isn't how things work in real life. Effective teachers try different approaches and repeat lessons before they expect a student to truly understand a topic. Or, sometimes a student must gain additional knowledge outside the classroom before they can contextualize and learn what the teacher was conveying.

I want to highlight the distinction between teaching and learning because it can be incredibly helpful for potty training. As a parent, you're trying to teach your child toilet independence, but it is up to the child to learn the lesson. Your child may learn right away, or they may need you to take a different approach and repeat the lessons. Or perhaps they may need to master other skills before their learning process is complete.

This can be a challenging revelation for some parents. Potty training is usually the first-time parents are confronted with the teaching/learning divide. Up to now, your child has likely progressed with their developmental milestones more or less independently. You naturally showed patience and understanding as you watched your child learn to walk, because you knew it was a milestone that takes time to develop. Since physical skills unfold intuitively without much direct instruction, you trust the process and allow your child to learn at their own pace. Sure, you've provided them with support and guidance, but you're not buying handbooks on how to teach your child to roll over. Those milestones happen without direct instruction and without much parental intervention.

Parental Involvement Stages

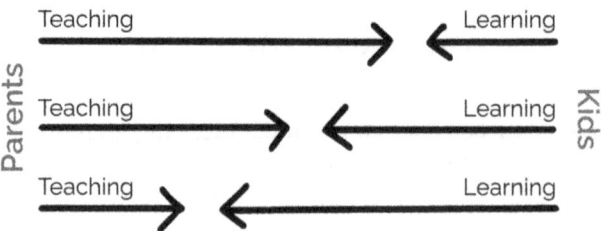

Potty training is different. There are so many steps our children must learn, and these things need to be taught. The good news? This is a super cool opportunity to learn more about your child! Through the potty-training process, you can get so many insights into their personality, temperament, and the way they learn. And as we get into the nuts and bolts of the *Good to Go* process, you'll see where you can tweak your teaching approach to meet your child's specific learning needs.

Values-Centered Parenting

My Values-Centered Parenting (VCP) approach is the first thing I teach in my parenting courses, regardless of the children's ages in the class. The beauty of this model is that it works for all families and for all situations. Once you understand and internalize this concept, you can apply this tool to any challenge.

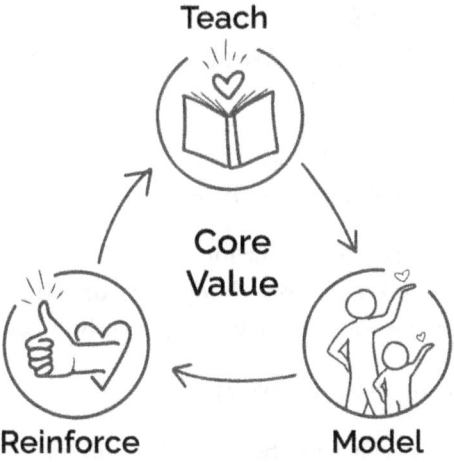

Values-Centered Parenting Tool

In an abstract sense, here is how you use the tool:

1. *Identify the core value* that is important to your family.
2. *Teach* your child.
3. *Model and narrate* the desired behavior.
4. *Reinforce* the desired behavior.
5. *Repeat* steps 2–4 as necessary.

If this seems overwhelming, remember that you are already doing this! The sheer act of parenting means you're constantly in some position on this VCP cycle. You are modeling even when you don't realize it, teaching every time you say something, and reinforcing whenever you pay attention to a behavior. But by being intentional about using the VCP, you can make sure your actions are in alignment with your core values.

Let's apply this with a real example of a common toddler challenge:

My child hates their car seat and fights getting the seatbelt on!

1. *Identify the core value* that is important to your family.
   Safety

2. *Teach* your child.
   Here we tell our child, "We put our seatbelts on to keep our bodies safe!"

3. *Model and narrate* the desired behavior.
   "Mommy is putting on her seatbelt to keep her body safe, too!"

4. *Reinforce* the desired behavior.
   "Look at you keeping your body safe!" or "Wow, you buckled that all by yourself, you're keeping your body safe!"

5. *Repeat* steps 2–4 as necessary.

This simple model can truly be applied to any parenting situation. The car-seat example is usually a no-brainer, because most parents wouldn't dream of letting their child ride in a car unbuckled. However, step 1, *identify the core value*, isn't going to be the same for every family.

Here's an example for the same problem, but with a different core value:

My child hates their car seat and fights getting the seatbelt on!

1. *Identify the core value* that is important to your family.
   Obedience

2. *Teach* your child.
   Here we tell our child, "The rules say we must be buckled up or we can't drive."

3. *Model and narrate* the desired behavior.
   "Mommy is also putting on her seatbelt so we don't get a ticket!"

4. *Reinforce* the desired behavior.
   "Look at you being so responsible!!" or "Wow, you buckled that all by yourself, you're such a good rule follower!"

5. *Repeat* steps 2–4 as necessary.
   The end result is the same (both kids got buckled up), but the core value is different.

HOW LAURA IS USING VCP TO AVOID TRIPS TO URGENT CARE

A big challenge in our house is getting my two boys to play nicely together. My older son, Auggie, often doesn't understand how his bigger size gives him an unfair advantage. Similarly, my toddler, Sebastian, doesn't have the impulse control yet to avoid lashing out when angry.

As you can imagine, this means playtime often ends in tears for one or both of them. I'm like any mom: when I hear my baby in pain, I flip into protective mama bear mode. The first few times one of my boys hurt the other, my instinct was to angrily lecture the offending party about why that was unacceptable behavior. Do you know what doesn't work with young kids? Long, angry lectures, it turns out. Pulling the aggressor aside and huffily explaining to him that what he did was wrong was not getting through.

Thankfully I remembered Gia's teachings and decided to work out how to handle these situations with the VCP tool.

What is the core value I'm trying to teach? When I thought about it, it was that we treat others with kindness and respect. Intentionally or unintentionally hurting a person's body or feelings isn't kind or respectful.

How can I teach this to the boys? Any chance I get, I bring up gentle touch, respecting body boundaries, and kindness. We read books about all these topics and practice how to tell others we need space or something hurt our feelings.

What kind of modeling can I do? If I accidentally bump into the kids or they tell me something I did hurt their feelings, I get down on their level and sincerely apologize. We have two cats, so I'll always narrate how I'm respecting their bodies when I need to move them off the couch (or the kitchen table, even if I'm irritated). When one of my boys gets hurt by the other, instead of lecturing the guilty party I instead focus on the injured or sad child. I empathize with them and model what kind of repair behavior I'd like to see happen in the future, but I don't lecture or force my other child to do what I'm doing.

Where can I reinforce this value? Children really are sponges, and my sons picked up on our teaching and modeling very quickly. When I see them apologizing and checking in with each other after an injury, I give them effusive and sincere praise right away. I will also bring up the kind acts later on, during bedtime or some quiet snuggles. I will tell them, "when you checked in with your brother, apologized, and gave him a big hug, I was so proud of you. You were so kind."

Teach
- Read books
- Practice gentle hands
- Conversations about kindness and body boundaries

Core Value: Kindness

Model
- Sincere apologies
- Gentle with our pets
- Narrating repairs

Reinforce
Notice and mention:
- Being kind to each other
- Petting the cat softly
- Giving me gentle hugs

Is my house now a perfectly serene haven full of eternally happy siblings? Of course not! (This morning, they were both on the floor crying because they wanted to sit in the same chair.) But the VCP tool gives me a simple rubric to fall back on, rather than reverting to a fight-or-flight mama bear.

Upskilling Is Magic

"My son was always happy at mealtime, but all of a sudden he's crying and throwing his food from his high chair."

"My daughter used to love bath time, but now she's crying and refusing to get in the bath every night!"

Do you see anything in common about the two statements above? These are two of the most common scenarios parents will recount to me during troubleshooting sessions, but it's not the specifics of the complaints that jump out at me.

Here's what I hear:

- She "used to" do something, and now she doesn't.
- He is "all of a sudden" not happy.

As a parenting educator, these phrases are a big indicator that it's time to utilize one of my favorite tools: upskilling.

Children are constantly learning and changing. We know this intellectually, but as parents, it's so reassuring to get into a groove with caretaking. Parenting is so hard—of course we're going to look for every opportunity to just keep a good thing going. So if your kid has always happily been strapped into the car seat, or been eating contentedly in her high chair, you're not going to rock the boat by changing up routines.

Of course, your kids have different plans for you. They often change overnight without us noticing, and that's when you'll notice things they "used to" do with no problems are "all of a sudden" a big pain point.

These are signs that your child needs upskilling. These new behaviors and attitudes (often interpreted as "misbehaviors" or "bad attitudes") are their way of saying "I'm not a baby anymore!" They've likely gotten a big software upgrade in their brains, and they need to be challenged at the next level. Instead of trying to get your child to behave as they used to, parents need to give them the next level of independence and control.

If you think of skills as a staircase, this concept might become more clear. At the bottom, you have where they are now, and at the top is the adult-level skill you're trying to teach.

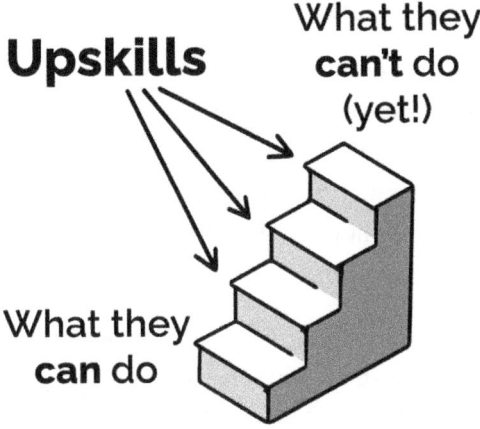

Maybe your toddler is currently in a high chair, set away from the table. Eventually, we'd like them to be adults who sit at tables willingly, eating their meals happily with friends and family. How do we get there? By taking steps up the skill staircase, right? Without these graduated steps, how will anyone learn independence and autonomy?

I'm going to geek out here a little bit on early childhood development. This Upskilling concept draws from Lev Vygotsky's Zone of Proximal Development (ZPD). The ZPD is the range between what a learner can do independently and what they can achieve with guidance from a more knowledgeable person. Scaffolding, according to Vygotsky, involves providing structured support tailored to the learner's abilities, gradually fading as the individual gains competence, fostering independent mastery of tasks within their ZPD. Vygotsky imagines this as a scaffold on a building that gets removed once the structure is built. I prefer the staircase visual, as it's more accessible and feels more applicable for young kids. Toddler parents will have to wait a long time before their children are ready to remove all the scaffolding (our frontal lobes aren't fully developed until our mid-twenties, after all), but we can climb the staircase much faster and easier.

In the example scenarios, this might mean:

- More control around bath time: letting her start the water herself, pick out which toys she brings in, or maybe even decide to shower instead of soaking in the tub
- More maturity at mealtime: taking the tray off the high chair and pulling it right up to the table, or moving to a booster seat

I love watching a parent's face when I first introduce the concept of upskilling. They usually give me the most skeptical, and often terrified, look. In fact, this exact example gets some of the best reactions in class—when I suggest they remove the tray and pull the baby up to the dining table, you'd think I had suggested giving the child keys to the family car instead! And I get it! Upskilling can be scary, especially for first-time parents. But one thing I know about children, especially toddlers, is that we often underestimate their capabilities.

With upskilling, instead of underestimating their capabilities, you instead set your goals even higher. More often than not, they will surprise you with their ability to meet these higher expectations.

Can't do (yet!):
Sitting in a dining chair

Booster seat
Remove tray
Pull high chair to table

Upskills

Can do:
Eat in a high chair

CAR-SEAT CONUNDRUMS

My first introduction to upskilling happened when Auggie was about fourteen months old. I was in Gia's class, and during troubleshooting time, I brought up how he used to love car rides but suddenly hated getting in the car seat.

Gia, of course, heard the key words: *used to* and *suddenly*.

The main problem was getting Auggie buckled into his *car* seat. Seemingly overnight, he had gone from a docile passenger to a screaming banshee who fought against the seat with super-human strength. (Seriously, how are one-year-olds that strong?!)

Gia's suggestion was to introduce upskilling when it came to getting into his car seat. She suggested allowing him to climb into the car seat on his own and letting him buckle the chest clip himself. Of course, my knee-jerk reaction was a wholesale rejection of the idea. This child was arching his back and throwing a massive fit whenever I tried to sit him down. I thought there was no way he would willingly climb into the seat on his own.

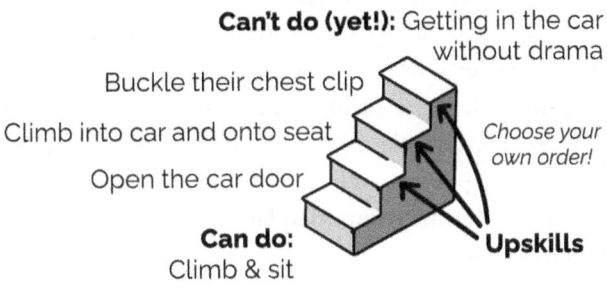

Thankfully, I trusted Gia's expertise more than I feared my volatile toddler, so I reluctantly gave it a try on the way home from class. I was fully expecting Auggie to spend twenty minutes playing around in the car, avoiding the actual task at hand. But, when I told him "Auggie, do you want to climb in all by yourself?" he instantly lit up and headed for his car seat. It was a bit of a struggle for him to get all the way up to the seat, but he enjoyed the challenge and was then super excited to buckle his chest clip (that one took a few tries).

The fact that these new tasks were just above his current skill level made them new and exciting for him. I was impressed to see him rise to the challenge, and he was newly engaged in the activity. Car rides became a lot more pleasant from that point on. Thanks, upskilling!

Descriptive versus Evaluative Praise

While it's wonderful that parents want to celebrate their children, not all praise is created equal.

When your child does something wonderful, it's natural to want to heap accolades on them. "Good job, baby! I'm so proud of you!" Isn't that supposed to build up their self esteem?

But child development experts warn that showering children with this kind of "evaluative praise" can be ineffective and possibly detrimental to their sense of inner motivation. This idea isn't new; after all, there are countless internet memes about parents being chastised for saying "good job!" But despite being a bit of a joke in the current zeitgeist, this recommendation to avoid evaluative praise is based on research.

The goal isn't to avoid praise altogether. Of course we want our children to know we love them, appreciate their efforts, and are amazed at their progress. The trick is in *how* we praise them.

This is where descriptive praise comes in. Some key elements of Descriptive praise include:

- Praising the effort, not the results
- Delivering praise in a calm, casual voice (rather than an exclamation)

- Noticing and describing the behavior, not the child
- Using praise to convey values and rules
- Being genuine and not exaggerated

Here's a shorthand to help you remember how to use descriptive praise: simply notice and mention. Here are some examples to help you get a hold of this:

If your child shows you a new drawing:

- Evaluative praise: "That's beautiful!"
- Descriptive praise: "Look at all the colors you chose, they're so lifelike. I notice it's very detailed."

If your child helps you carry in groceries:

- Evaluative praise: "You're awesome!"
- Descriptive praise: "Wow, that was a heavy load. Thank you for helping me carry it in."

If your child adjusts their speaking volume when inside:

- Evaluative praise: "Good job!"
- Descriptive praise: "You're using your inside voice, thank you for protecting our ears."

When you first hear descriptive praise, it may sound weird! Most of us were raised with evaluative praise and can find descriptive praise cold or clinical. But, as you practice it with your child, you'll notice how effective it can become. After all, the goal of praise is to help your child learn what behaviors to replicate, and there's nothing useful or actionable in the phrase "good job!" But if they hear, "wow, you were very focused to finish that coloring page," they actually feel seen and know what behavior (focusing) is considered praiseworthy.

Now, does this mean you can never tell your child "good job!" ever again? Of course not! This is not about being the language police;

we're just working toward adding in more and more descriptive praise until it becomes second nature.

Natural and Logical Consequences

Natural consequences are things that just happen. They're a type of consequence that doesn't require parental intervention. The classic example is a child who doesn't want to wear a coat in the dead of winter. No matter how much you try to convince them to put it on, the child just (frustratingly) refuses to wear a coat. You know they're not going to get frostbite if they go outside—they'll be safe, just uncomfortable. The natural consequence is simply that they will feel cold. So you decide to allow them to go outside in shirtsleeves and tell them what to expect. "Okay, we can go outside without your coat, but you'll probably be very cold." With the narration and experience of going outside, the hope is that they'll connect this discomfort with their choice to reject the coat and make a better choice next time (or ask for their dang coat back!).

A logical consequence is something that requires parental intervention, but makes sense based on the situation. Take the same scenario as above, where your child doesn't want to wear a coat. A parent can take into account how cold it actually is and whether it's safe to allow a child to experience the natural consequence of going outside. But if it's unsafe to go out underdressed (or, say, you don't feel comfortable with the scorn of passersby judging your parenting), you can choose to employ a logical consequence. A logical consequence in this situation is that your child can't go play outside without their coat. "It is too cold, so it's unsafe to go outside without your coat. If you don't put it on, we will stay inside." The idea is that, even though the "discipline" is parent-led, it is not arbitrary or illogical. The goal of logical consequences is to help children develop self control, internal understanding, and a desire to follow the rules.

By the way, these consequences can be positive as well. If your child does choose to wear the coat, you can highlight the consequences of their choice for them. "I bet you feel warm and cozy in that coat, I think it's so cool how you chose to put it on!" or "I bet you're so glad you chose to wear the coat, it's fun playing in the snow!"

These two types of consequences contrast with illogical consequences, which are consequences that are both created by the parent and don't make a lot of sense in the situation. Though sometimes necessary, these types of consequences feel arbitrary and unfair for kids and make it more difficult for them to develop self-motivation. (After all, if you have no idea what the consequence is for an action, how can you plan for the future?) An illogical consequence in the coat scenario could be something like taking away screen time if they don't put on the coat.

But before we jump to consequences, the first step will be to start with empathy. The phrase "I've noticed that" is a great place to start—it allows for a simple, nonjudgmental observation that may give kids a clue of what's going on.

"I've noticed that you don't like putting on your coat."

Then move on to frame the problem:

"I wonder if there's something you don't like about your coat that we can fix?"

This is where your child may disclose that the coat is itchy, or they don't like the color, or that they get too sweaty while wearing it. If something fixable comes to light, you've managed to jump over the consequence step and move on with your day. Giving your child some agency in the decision, even if it's just picking a different coat, can make them feel more in control and more willing to cooperate.

But let's say this is the only winter coat that fits your kid, and there's no quick fix. Now we move on to the consequences described above.

The Negotiation Sequence

I'm not sure why the word "negotiation" has gotten such a bad reputation in parenting circles. You see it all over: blog posts telling you to stop negotiating with your toddler, or parenting experts on social media admonishing you for engaging in negotiation with your kids. Maybe this is a remnant from the more authoritarian parenting of yore, where the adults were expected to be infallible dictators and children either fell in line or were labeled as "disobedient."

I think what's more likely is that we are negotiating out of order. A parent will set a boundary, then a child will "negotiate" by whining or melting down, and then a parent gives in. By setting a hard boundary from the start, a parent gives themselves no wiggle room to compromise. If they end up meeting their child in the middle, the compromise becomes capitulation instead.

And while we have all picked our battles with our kids, and given in when needed, doing this repeatedly teaches your child that your boundaries aren't important.

I am highlighting this topic because you will likely find yourself negotiating with your child during the potty-training process, possibly multiple times a day. Learning a better way to negotiate will allow you to bypass power struggles and keep the peace.

By understanding their triggers and anticipating common power struggles, you can help your child feel more in control, while maintaining parental authority. Clearly explaining expectations and future events can help a child feel more grounded and in control. And while children have a deep desire for autonomy, they also need a sense of containment. Kids don't like being told exactly what to do, but they also don't like unfettered freedom.

This usually comes into play during transition times. A simple example is when it's time to leave a playground. Kids usually don't want to stop playing and aren't going to willingly leave. You could attempt to prevent a power struggle by offering them a very simple choice: "It's time to leave! Would you like to walk to the car or should I carry you?" Sometimes, just offering this simple choice is enough.

But what if they reject both choices? "Nooo! I don't want to leave!!!" You could just jump straight to forcing them to leave and carry them out kicking and screaming. But first, in an attempt to find compromise and preserve their sense of autonomy, I'd recommend trying this method of negotiating with your child. Just like a math problem, the order of operations is important here, so make sure you follow each step in order. Here's the three-step sequence I teach parents.

Step 1: Share Perspectives

This is the *connection* step of the process. We're trying to get your child to see you as a collaborator and as someone with their own autonomous wants and needs.

In order to do this, we're going to use "I" statements to explore each of your perspectives. Continuing the example from above, you could say, "I hear that you REALLY don't want to leave the park." Then add in your own perspective. "I want to leave because it's dinnertime and I'm hungry!" Now, you encourage them to repeat back what they hear as you had just done for them. It may not happen right away, but the goal is for them to say, "Mommy wants to leave, mommy is hungry." You may have to prompt them, "Can you tell me what you just heard? How do I feel right now? What do I want?"

Kids often conflate paraphrasing your words with agreement. We want to teach our kids that just because they're reflecting our feelings back at us, that doesn't mean they have to agree with us. Our main goal is to ensure mutual understanding of each other's perspective before moving on.

This is an excellent opportunity to teach your child listening skills in a positive light. Often, our kids only hear the word "listening" in a negative context: "You're not listening to me!" Here, we can ask for our child's perspective and reflect back, "Wow, I'm listening, and I hear what you're saying." This models active listening and will support your child's ability to reciprocate.

Step 2: Teach Compromise

The aim here is to establish a shared goal where both parent and child feel valued and respected within the family structure. Compromise isn't about splitting things equally; it's more about *equity* and mutual respect. Encourage your kid to share their thoughts and brainstorm a solution together.

> Parent: "Now that we understand how each other is feeling, what should we do?"
> Child: "Stay at the park!"
> Parent: "That's only what you want, but it doesn't help me! I'm still hungry."
> Child: "I want to keep playing."
> Parent: "Here's an idea, what if we pick one more activity before we go. Do you want to do the slides or the swings before we leave? A little bit of what you want, and a little bit of what I want."
> Child: "Swings!"

So far, this isn't a zero-sum game. There's no "winner" or "loser," you're just working with your child to come up with a solution.

Step 3: Seal the Deal

Now that you've come to a compromise, it's time to seal the deal. This is, arguably, the most important part of the negotiation. I like solidifying the agreement with something symbolic, like a handshake, which helps bring the compromise out of the realm of abstract thinking and into the real world, taking it from an abstract concept to a concrete plan. "Okay, we're going to swing twenty times and then it's time to go. Deal? Let's shake on it!"

The Negotiation Sequence

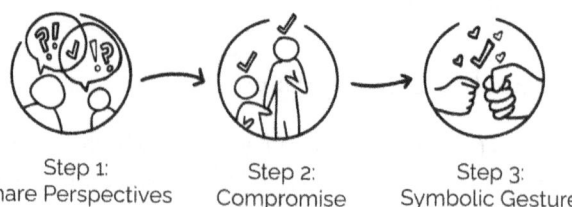

Step 1: Share Perspectives   Step 2: Compromise   Step 3: Symbolic Gesture

After sealing the deal, consider this written in stone. Before the handshake, there's wiggle room for negotiation. But afterward, this is a boundary you are not going to change or break, no matter what happens. This is why the order is so important. Your child may very well melt down and protest after those twenty swings, even though you went through this whole process with them. You may still have to carry them kicking and screaming out of the park after all.

If you're new to this process, or new to holding boundaries with your kids, you're not going to see overnight behavior changes from implementing this. It may take up to nine times of implementing this negotiation sequence for any issues that arise before it finally clicks that you stick to your boundaries. But by establishing this routine of negotiation, then holding the boundary, you will eventually see your power struggles reduce significantly.

I want you to keep these three steps in mind for future potty-training negotiations—we'll be revisiting them for the inevitable power struggles that come with the process.

Creating an Emotional Hygiene Routine

Just like we take care of our physical hygiene by brushing our teeth and taking baths, our emotional health benefits from routine care. You don't wait until your teeth start aching to brush them, so why would you wait for a meltdown to address your thoughts and feelings? Taking care of our emotions on a daily basis helps us develop regulation skills and can give your child valuable coping skills that will serve them for the rest of their lives.

Pick a predictable time each day when you can practice for one to five minutes (any longer will be too much for young children). Find a cozy space in your home that can be dedicated to this practice, or set up a "cozy corner" in your child's playroom or bedroom filled with blankets, pillows, and their favorite stuffed animals. In this dedicated space and time, you introduce strategies to help your child learn emotional regulation.

Teach your child some practical methods for calming down their central nervous system. There are tangible and intangible tools you can utilize to help them regulate their emotions.

Tangible tools include:

- Children's books about emotional regulation
- Weighted blankets / body socks
- Emotion charts
- Coloring books and crayons / markers / colored pencils
- Blank notebooks for "journaling" (even if your child can't write)
- Inspirational cards
- Chimes, bells, or singing bowls
- Aromatherapy, candles, or incense
- Calming fidgets like two-way sequined pillows or pop-it toys

Intangible tools include:

- Positive affirmations
- Meditation
- Deep breaths
- Music
- Mantras or call and response affirmations
- Gentle movement or yoga
- Pressure point massage
- Progressive muscle relaxation

With your child, you can use these tools to practice one specific emotional-regulation strategy every day. It's important to practice these skills repeatedly at neutral times, when your child isn't experiencing big feelings. With enough practice, your child will be able to access these strategies like muscle memory when they're really needed.

Chapter in Review

- There is a fundamental difference between teaching and learning.
- VCP is a foundational tool that can be used for any parenting issue. Parenting is a constant cycle of teaching, modeling, and reinforcing around your core values and beliefs.
- Upskilling is about setting the bar higher than your child's current abilities, to allow them to stretch and grow. "Used to" and "all of a sudden" are key phrases that indicate it's time to upskill.
- Descriptive praise is the best way to increase desired behavior. Simply notice and mention the behaviors you want to see flourish.
- Natural consequences require no intervention while logical consequences are imposed by the parent, but make sense in the moment—both types of consequences are useful for learning. Avoid illogical consequences if you can.
- Negotiation is not a bad word. Teaching your child how to listen and compromise is a lifelong tool.
- Emotional hygiene is as important as physical hygiene. Creating a one- to five-minute daily practice can go a long way!

3

Rethinking Readiness

Okay, so at this point you may be thinking: "Sure, this all sounds great and may be useful for potty learning, but what if my kid just isn't ready yet?"

We hear about "readiness for potty training" in almost every resource out there. Some methods suggest your child needs to check every box of a skills checklist before starting. Others pick arbitrary ages where they insist it's not just ideal, but imperative to start using the potty. These books will tell you that if you're one month younger or a day older than their prescribed window, you'll end up with a lifetime of potty problems.

In my experience, none of this is true. First, there's no magic age for potty learning—every child is different and requires a personalized approach. There are averages and trends that we can look at, but your child is not a statistic or a trend.

And while there are many developmental signs of readiness for toilet independence, I think these have been overemphasized by other potty-training manuals. With the *Good to Go* method, we're not all that concerned if your child is showing these readiness behaviors because we're more focused on helping them learn through observation and exposure and building up their capabilities.

Some Skills Are Teachable, Some Are Not

While I don't think there's a finite list of prerequisites for potty training, there are some clear signs that may indicate your child will be successful. These signs fall into two categories: teachable and non-teachable.

Teachable skills are developmentally appropriate skills you can help your child learn.

Non-teachable skills are based on developmental milestones that will happen regardless of your child's willingness to participate.

A simple example of this dichotomy can be found in learning how to ride a bike. A child may be ready to ride a bike based on their gross motor development, balance, and coordination around ages three to four. But to help them be capable of riding independently, parents need to teach them specific skills like how to put on a helmet, balance on the bike seat, and push the pedals.

Understanding the difference between developmental readiness and temperamental capability is going to be really helpful during potty training. Knowing which signs are developmental and which are teachable will allow you to make an informed decision about when to start.

Physical, Cognitive, and Social-Emotional

Let's take a closer look at the three domains of development to assess whether your child is ready to go diaper free: physical, cognitive, and social-emotional.

Physical Signs

A child showing all the physical signs of readiness will naturally have the bladder and bowel control to go longer stretches with a clean and dry diaper (see Table 3.1). You may also notice a predictable schedule for when they fill their diapers, like after breakfast and dinner, for example. They're also going to be pooping during awake hours only and often waking up completely dry from naps. Finally, they'll have enough core strength and coordination to sit on a chair without falling off.

Table 3.1 Physical Signs

Non-Teachable	Teachable
• Has sufficient bladder and bowel capacity and muscle control	• Can dress and undress independently (mostly)
• Eliminates predictably	• Adequately washes and dries hands independently
• Poops during the day (not while asleep)	• Can attempt to wipe themselves (not fully)
• Wakes up dry from naps	• Squats to poo
• Has sufficient balance and coordination to sit on a potty without falling off	

We can teach them the steps to dress and undress (pulling down pants and underwear are critical skills for the pottying process) and proper hand-washing hygiene. And while we don't expect kids to be fully independent at wiping until around age five, now is an opportunity to start working toward that goal by attempting a wipe and then having the parent finish the job. And we'll be talking more about this later in this chapter, but one big thing you can teach is getting your child into the squatting position while pooping.

Cognitive Signs

Your toddler may be getting extra curious about what's happening when you go to the potty (see Table 3.2). Maybe when they get into the bath they freeze and stare because they've noticed they're peeing. It's also clear they're understanding almost everything you're telling them and attempting to communicate back with words or signs. They're also able to follow multi-step directions like "pick up your diaper and take it to the trash." And finally, you've noticed they're developing memories that stick around for longer: maybe they're bringing up stuff that happened last week or last month.

Table 3.2 Cognitive Signs

Non-Teachable	Teachable
• Shows interest in your potty habits	• Uses accurate language for elimination
• Freezes when going #1	• Discloses to you before, during, or after
• Has robust receptive language and blossoming expressive language	• Follows 2–5 steps of the toileting sequence
• Can follow 1–2 step directions	• Learns that water turns into pee and food turns into poo
• Demonstrates long-term memory and retention	

This is the time when we can start teaching them specific words to use around elimination—you get to choose what those are for your family, all that matters is that you're consistent with the words you use. You can also help them learn how to tell you about potty events, whether it's before, during, or after. Here is where we'll start teaching them some of the steps of the *Good to Go* "Universal Potty Sequence" (more on that in Part II). Finally, you can teach them the simple biology lesson of how the food we eat turns into poop and the liquids turn into water!

Social-Emotional Signs

Many kids start hiding when it's time to poop—you'll find them crouching in a corner or going into a different room to do the deed in privacy (see Table 3.3). They may also ask to be changed right away, rather than sit in a wet or dirty diaper. You'll have noticed their emotions becoming more nuanced and complex: sadness mixed with anger, happiness mixed with nervousness, and so on. Also, if they start wanting to join you in the bathroom and begin asking questions or seem curious about how you go potty, this could be a good sign of readiness.

Table 3.3 Social-Emotional Signs

Non-Teachable	Teachable
• Hides for #2	• Emotional regulation: the ability to employ coping strategies for frustration and disappointment
• May want to be changed right away	• Can name feelings and seeks self- or co-regulation
• Has a range of complex emotions	• Smooth transitions in other scenarios
• Imitates "big kids" or parents going potty, or wants to join	

When you notice these signs, it's a good time to start teaching and modeling coping strategies for big feelings, especially around frustration or disappointment. (Potty training can be both these things, and it's good to practice emotional-regulation techniques before you start adding bodily excretions to the mix!) You can also help them learn how to name their feelings and seek co-regulation with you or another adult. Finally, one common challenge in potty training is the kid who doesn't want to stop playing to use the toilet. Now is the time to start working on smooth transitions between activities so they'll be more practiced at it when it really matters!

Remember, the items in the left column aren't teachable, and most children won't show all these signs. And that's okay! *Signs of readiness are not prerequisites!* Instead, think of them as raffle tickets: the more you have, the more likely you are to win the big prize. If you notice many of these signs of readiness (usually starting around eighteen months), it could be a good indication that it's time to start on the potty-training path.

The capabilities listed in the right column are things we should be helping our children learn during this process. You can do this any time, even if you're not ready to officially start potty training yet.

Understanding Early Development

Check in with yourself for a moment: did reading that laundry list of skills and abilities in the previous section bring up some anxiety? So many parents are perpetually worried about developmental milestones, and it's normal to be concerned by (and pay close attention to) how your child is progressing.

Before you become a parent, you may expect these milestones to appear at regular intervals—after all, that's what your pediatrician's handout told you! At your child's appointment, they hand you a chart with all the different skills you can expect your child to display in the coming months and send you on your merry way. There may be a column that says "physical" and another that says "social-emotional," and a list of all the things your child should be doing by their next checkup.

But what they don't tell you is that these things don't all happen at the same time. In fact, they rarely do. Most early childhood development is asynchronous, as in "out of sync," or not simultaneous. Across the different domains—physical, cognitive, and social-emotional—development happens at different rates.

What this means, in practice, is that your child may surge ahead in one domain, while appearing to be "behind" in another.

For example, you may have watched your child be laser-focused on learning to walk around their first birthday. During that time, all their attention and energy was going toward mastering this gross motor skill. But, at the same time, you may have worried about your child's speaking abilities. Maybe they weren't talking as much as you had expected, and you started to get worried about their language milestones falling behind.

Then, around eighteen months, seemingly overnight, your child had an explosion of new words. For the previous six months, you had fretted over their language acquisition, and then, all of a sudden, they're little chatterboxes.

Even if the particulars of this scenario may not resonate with you, if you look back at your child's developmental progress, I'm sure you can find examples of their own asynchronous development. It's almost as if these kids need to concentrate on one area of development at a time, while the others pause or slow down temporarily. As parents, it's important to remember that when a child is mastering one skill, it doesn't mean they're behind in another—rather, they're shifting their energy.

How does this apply to potty training? Well, if you recall, I made a point to say that the signs of readiness are not prerequisites—your child does not need to check all the boxes to be ready for potty training. This is because all their development isn't going to be caught up to the same point, especially if you're starting on the younger side.

Also, it's important to recognize that potty training takes a lot of effort. Your child is going to be engrossed in learning this new, important life skill. During this time of intensive focus and learning, your child may need to unconsciously put other developmental skills on the back burner.

Understanding Body Awareness

One major clue to your child's readiness is figuring out where they are in developing their own body awareness. The scientific term for it is "interoception," the physiological sense that allows you to perceive and interpret internal signals from your body. This includes sensations like hunger, thirst, and (most importantly for potty training) digestive and bladder signals. Many of us have never thought much about our body's signals—as adults, we move through the world with most of our body-awareness cues on autopilot.

Small children, on the other hand, have to learn how to interpret these feelings before they can translate them into action. And it's a lot to process! Imagine what a pang of hunger feels like: for me, it's like a hollow, almost sour ache. As an adult, I instantly know that feeling means it's time to eat. But for babies, it takes time for them to connect that feeling with the necessary action of eating. And it takes many repetitions of feeling hunger, then having it resolve after eating, before they connect the two actions. Only once they make this internal connection can they develop the ability to communicate to their parents that they're hungry.

When it comes to pottying, children's interoception skills progress through predictable stages. For example, do they know they've peed, or are they unaware?

While the early stages of potty awareness are developmental, once kids get to the "I'm peeing!" stage, we can start teaching them to connect the feeling to the needed action (e.g., running to the potty!) (see Table 3.4).

Table 3.4 Progression of Potty Awareness

Unaware	I went?	I'm going!	I need to go!
0–18 months	18–24 months	+/– 2 years	+/– 2 years
Doesn't seem bothered by full diapers; not showing visual cues of elimination	Pulls at diaper; wants to be changed right away; walks differently with full diaper	Freezes when peeing; hides to go poop; announces as it's happening	Discloses or announces need; looks panicked; grabs diaper; asks for help

What about Nighttime Dryness?

While most kids stop pooping overnight by the time they're toddlers, this doesn't hold true for pee. Nighttime dryness is not teachable—it's actually a neurological milestone. It may seem frustratingly slow, but we just have to wait for their brain development to get to this point. Rarely, a toddler will start staying dry overnight before they master daytime potty training, but this is the exception—most children take much longer. It's actually completely normal for children to continue peeing at night up to age eight. Many pediatricians won't even consider bedwetting a "problem" until age nine. In my educated opinion, potty-training resources that endorse "night training" are not evidence-based and cause more harm than good. Because of this, *Good to Go* only focuses on potty training during waking hours. This is why we do not include nighttime dryness as a prerequisite or a sign of daytime training (Table 3.5).

Though we won't be focusing on nighttime dryness during the first phase of potty training, I'll give you some tips on how to know when it's time to remove nighttime diapers in Part II.

Table 3.5 Nighttime Dryness by the Numbers

Age	Wetness rates
5	About 1 in 6 children
6	About 1 in 8 children
7	About 1 in 10 children
15	1–2 in 100 children

Okay... So When Should I Start?

There's no hard-and-fast rule about when you should start potty training. Every child is going to be different, and sometimes it's just a gut decision by parents.

That said, I know you want something definitive! So, I've created this decision-making flowchart to help you decide if it's the right time for your child. I've based this info off developmental averages and my experience as a teacher, and I think it will be a helpful guide for most families.

You can follow the chart on the next page, or read through these questions:

1. Is there a deadline within two months?

    Yes: Start! They're good to go!

    No: Continue to question 2.

2. Is my child twenty-four months or older?

    Yes: Continue to question 3.

    No: Wait to start until they're at least two years old.

3. Are they in stage 3 or 4 of sensation awareness? (Either "I'm peeing!" or "I need to pee!")

    Yes: Continue to question 4.

    No: Jump to question 5.

4. Are they showing one to two non-teachable signs from each category?

    Yes: Start! They're good to go!

    No: Continue to question 5.

5. Are they three years old or older?

    Yes: Start now! They're good to go!

    No: Wait until you see one to two non-teachable signs from each category.

Should I start?

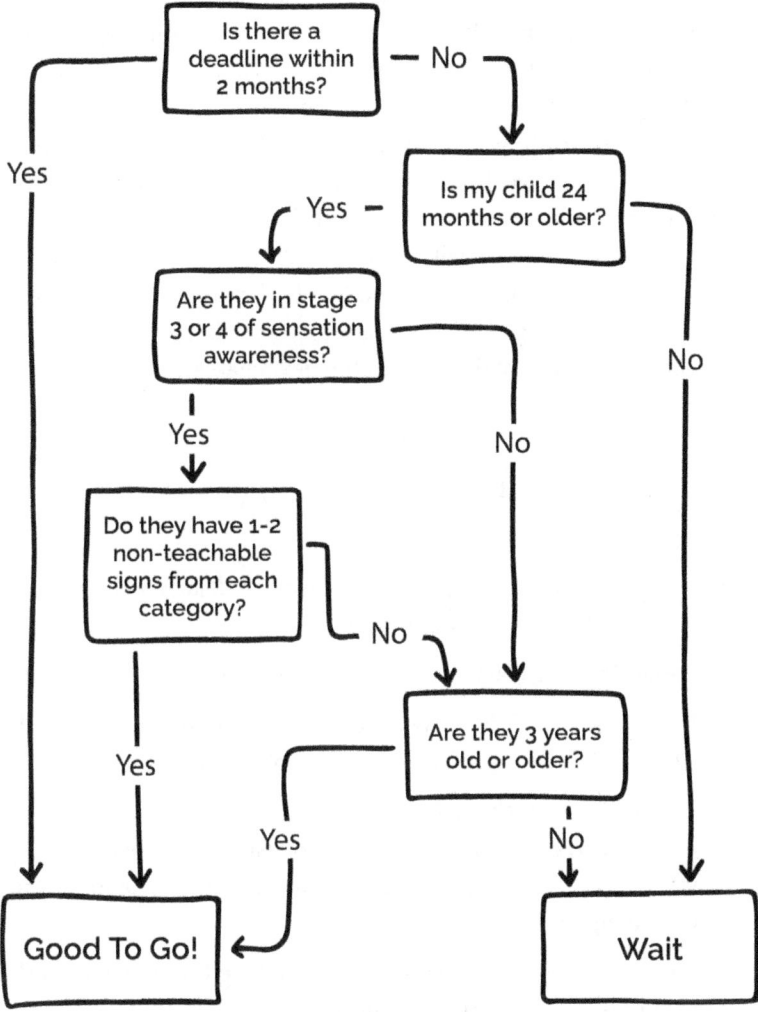

Remember, these questions are only supposed to act as general guidelines. You may need to adjust these ages if your child was premature, or if they have a developmental disability.

What If This Isn't Your First Rodeo?

If you're coming to the *Good to Go* method after already trying a different approach to potty training, that's totally okay. First of all: nobody's grading you. This isn't a test. This parenting thing often requires trial and error, and I don't think anyone should be shamed for tackling problems from a variety of angles.

But if you're reading this book, I'm guessing whatever you tried before hasn't been working, and that's okay, too! The big-picture parenting tools found in *Good to Go* don't have an expiration date and can be used to build upon whatever your child has already learned.

Even if your child has developed habits that are actively working against potty training, you can start to re-teach the fundamentals using the techniques we describe in the next chapter.

Chapter in Review

- Looking for elusive signs of readiness can delay you from starting the potty-training journey.
- Some skills are teachable, while others are not.
- Non-teachable skills: developmental milestones you can't rush, such as bladder capacity, bowel control, and nighttime dryness.
- Teachable skills: these are skills you can actively teach your child, like recognizing the urge to go, using potty-related vocabulary, following the steps involved in using the toilet, and practicing hygiene.
- Focus on what teachable skills you can help build in your child to successfully enter potty training.
- There are three domains of development to consider: physical, cognitive, and social-emotional.

- Asynchronous development is normal. While children are busy learning one new skill, other skills sometimes take a backseat.
- Children progress through stages from unaware to anticipation.
- Nighttime dryness is not teachable and not necessary for daytime training.

4

Are YOU Ready?

So much of the parenting journey does not involve choice. We don't get to choose the timing of big milestones like walking or the subsequent challenges that come with it! When your child first started walking, and they were suddenly able to get into everything, you had to adjust accordingly—installing locks on cabinets, gating off the stairs, and putting plug covers on the outlets. At first, it may have been stressful, but eventually you learned to love watching them explore the world in new ways.

Potty training is different because parents have a huge amount of choice. For the most part, you can choose the timing and the method and really shape how your child learns. But also, a parent must willingly *choose* to make their lives temporarily more difficult to help their child learn to use the potty.

The truth is, diapers are convenient. Unless there's a serious blowout, diapers buy you time and don't require you to stop what you're doing to go to the bathroom. Intentionally deciding to forgo diapers means you're actively choosing to be inconvenienced, at least for a time.

But just like babyproofing in your house, this is a temporary annoyance that leads to a greater good. At the very least, imagine not having to bring bulky diapers everywhere you go! (This is a huge improvement when it comes to traveling—think of all the luggage space you've just freed up for souvenirs!)

I'm bringing this up because, when it comes to potty training, your child's readiness is only one part of the equation. We also have to think about you, the parent or primary caregiver, and anyone else involved in caring for your child. It's no secret that potty training is a big transition, and it's important to acknowledge that you're going to intentionally make your life more challenging for a short while.

So, ask yourself: am I ready?

If the answer is no, reflect on the reason why.

Maybe it's simply logistical: you're about to have a new baby and you don't think you'll have the time, focus, and energy to fully engage in potty training. Great—wait until you're past the postpartum fog and start then. Or, if you have a partner, have them officially take ownership of potty training, acknowledging your own limitations at the moment.

Maybe you don't feel emotionally ready? It can be surprisingly emotional to see your baby start using a toilet like a big kid. This can bring up unexpected feelings in parents, and you may find yourself resisting potty training because you're not ready to see your child grow up so fast. Or maybe your own anxiety is getting the best of you, and you're so worried about the challenge of potty training that you'd rather just put it off indefinitely.

I'm here to validate you! This is a big deal, and it brings up big feelings. But now that you've recognized and named these feelings, I'm going to encourage you to work through them. It may help to talk with friends and family who have slightly older kids and who have been through this before. Finding someone you trust who can make you feel seen and supported is key.

The attitude that we, as parents, bring into potty training is just as important as what our child is bringing. By anticipating your own feelings and finding your own coping skills, you can set yourself up for success, too.

Plus, I know you can do this! I've coached hundreds of families through potty training, and I can confidently say that everybody survived the process. Plus, you're more capable and powerful than you even know. Heck, you survived the sleepless nights of the newborn phase, you are a rock star! You've got this potty training thing, trust me.

TWO KIDS IN DIAPERS IS . . . ?

As I mentioned in the introduction, I failed at potty training Auggie the first time around. One major reason it was a failure was because we started way too early. I now realize that he was showing a lot of the cognitive signs of readiness, but almost nothing in the other domains of development.

But another big reason I wanted to potty train him so early was because his little brother, Sebastian, was making an imminent arrival. And for some reason, I had thought it would be easier to have Auggie out of diapers before the baby arrived.

I'm not sure where I picked up this idea. I felt like it made sense—having two kids in diapers seemed like twice the work, right? Wouldn't it make sense to have one kid potty trained so we wouldn't have to deal with the expense and annoyance of both kids using diapers?

What I didn't realize was that, because Auggie was so young and not quite ready, I'd be stuck in the highly involved phase of potty training while also caring for a newborn.

Imagine: your partner is out grocery shopping. You've had ninety minutes of sleep in the past twenty-four hours, there's a tiny baby attached to your boob. Suddenly, you notice your older child doing the potty dance. You prompt them to go, but they're so engrossed in their Transformers toy it's unclear that they're even aware of your existence. What do you do? Do you: (a) unlatch the newborn so you can rush your toddler to the potty? Or do you: (b) let your kid pee on the floor and hope the cats don't walk through it before your nursing session is over?

For me; the answer was: (c) all of the above. Much to Sebastian's dismay, I paused his third breakfast and put him in the bouncer so I could rush Auggie to the potty. But I wasn't quick enough, and there was a shockingly huge amount of pee on the floor (he's always been very well hydrated, I'll give him that). In the ten seconds it took to grab a rag, my elderly and oblivious cat, Magnus, took a leisurely stroll right through the lake of urine and then jumped up on the couch.

I'm not telling you this story to dissuade you from potty training. But I just want you to learn from my mistakes. Don't potty train just because you think diapers are annoying.

Not long after this incident, we all decided to take a break on Auggie's potty training, and he started wearing daytime diapers again. It was only then that I realized how freaking convenient diapers actually are.

I now know that having two kids in diapers is both convenient and totally normal. I wish someone had just told me that when I was pregnant.

Potty Training Is Not a Light Switch

Recently, a mom approached me for help with her three-year-old son. Almost six months before, she had attempted an intensive, three-day potty training method and had proclaimed success! Though that first long weekend was messy and stressful, her son was using the toilet and wearing underwear by day four, and she patted herself on the back for finishing potty training.

But this wasn't the end of the story. She quickly realized that even though her son *knew* how to use the potty, he often wasn't making it in time. When she came to me for guidance, she sheepishly admitted that she had to remind her son to use the potty all the time, and that she had reverted to pull-ups for long car rides. She told me she felt like a failure because of these things and asked whether it meant that her son wasn't actually "potty trained" anymore?

So many parenting resources refer to potty training as a one-and-done situation. It's treated as a binary: you're either potty trained or you're not. And I see the appeal of thinking this difficult transition can happen quickly and completely almost overnight. But this black-and-white thinking isn't helpful and can cause so much shame and embarrassment for parents who think they've somehow "failed" potty training.

Instead, I want us to think of potty training as a *process* (see Table 4.1). When we start the process, parents are highly involved: actively teaching, reminding, and wiping butts. By the end of the process, parents are uninvolved: the entire process is done without any parental reminders or intervention.

It's unreasonable to expect our children to go through this process overnight. It's like handing a copy of *War and Peace* to a kindergartner who just learned to sound out words. Nobody expects perfect mastery from a new reader, so why do we hold toilet learning to a different standard?

I reassured this mom that she hadn't failed, but instead was just still in the highly involved phase of potty training. I also taught her some of the *Good to Go* techniques that would help her move on to the next phase of involvement, because the goal of the *Good to Go* method isn't to completely eliminate parental involvement, but to shorten the highly involved phase so we can all get on with our normal lives.

What follows are some considerations for adults to take into account before starting the potty-training process with their children.

Table 4.1 *Parental Involvement Stages*

Level of involvement	Supports	Typical duration
Highly involved	Providing frequent reminders, changing clothes after accidents, restricting activities/staying home to avoid accidents	A few days to weeks
Occasionally involved	Wiping after #2, providing occasional reminders, accompanying them in the stall in public restrooms, keeping spare clothes on hand in case of accidents	Up to age 5 or 6
Rarely involved	Encouraging bathroom visits before leaving the house, hygiene reminders (hand washing, proper wiping technique) without direct intervention	Until age 10+

Decide on Consistent Vocabulary

You and all other caregivers should agree on what you're going to call #1 and #2. It doesn't matter what it is, as long as it's consistent and respectful (please, no words that imply using the potty is shameful or dirty!). You should also pick words that you'll be comfortable using in public. If your child is in school, check with their teachers to see if they have preferred language they use so you can be on the same page.

Pregnancy or Adoption

If there's a new baby on the way, timing is key! Ideally, you'll want to give yourself at least two months of lead time before the baby arrives. This will give your toddler enough time to settle into their potty-training routine and become more comfortable (and predictable) with using the potty. You don't want your child to feel rushed or overwhelmed by starting too close to the due date.

If you have less than two months, I recommend waiting until after the baby is born (see the "Younger Siblings" heading in Chapter 6, "Set the Stage," for specific instructions). Remember, successful potty training depends on your child's stage of sensation awareness and non-teachable signs across domains: physical, cognitive, and social-emotional. So choose the timing that feels best for your family's needs!

Also, if you've started and then your baby arrives sooner than expected, it's okay to take a break and start again. Nobody is going to fault you for pausing the potty-training process to focus on a new baby, and your child won't forget everything just because you're going back to diapers. (More on this in Chapter 9, "Expect the Unexpected.")

Check for Underlying Conditions or Medical Issues

If your child is showing any unusual signs or symptoms, you should rule out medical problems before starting. For example, frequent urination can be a sign of type 1 diabetes, painful urination can be a sign of a urinary tract infection, and hard or infrequent poops can indicate constipation problems. Check with your child's pediatrician if you have any concerns or questions.

Get in Alignment

Consistency is key, so discuss your approach with all caregivers in your child's life. If you have a partner or co-parent, they'll be the most important person to help get aligned with the *Good to Go* method. Ideally, you'll both read this book together, but at the very least they should read the chapter summaries and discuss the game plan with you before starting. You may also need to consult with grandparents, aunts, uncles, nannies, or preschool teachers to make sure everyone can help support your child during this transition. The more adults who are able to consistently reinforce the lessons in *Good to Go*, the more chance your child has for success.

I've encouraged you to get the support of other adults in your life, but what if they don't have time to read *Good to Go*? It's ideal for everyone involved in the process to be consistent with how they approach potty training. This includes using the same terminology and teaching approaches and also knowing how to handle misses and do things like encouraging routine tries. This book contains a lot of specialized knowledge that is essential for potty training.

In many two-parent families, there is often one person who takes on the responsibility to do all the research and learning about parenting. Historically, this role would default to the mom, who ends up shouldering the burden of not just acquiring the information, but also being responsible for teaching this information to her partner. If you find yourself in this dynamic, I want to acknowledge that this is a lot of work and cognitive load to bear!

To help lessen the load, we've designed summaries that you'll find at the end of each chapter. These chapters in review should give everyone involved a sense of the approach and free you up to have more of a baseline to begin discussions about the process.

But if you find yourself in a position where other caregivers aren't willing to even read these summaries, I just want to acknowledge *you* and all the hard work *you* are putting into this! Your child is lucky to have a parent who cares so much about them and is willing to learn new skills in order to make their lives happier. Gold star for you!

High-Conflict Co-Parenting

First, I'd like to establish a distinction between co-parenting and sole-parenting. While being a sole-parent has many challenges, the upside is that you are the sole decision maker. Sole-parents provide all the resources and as a result they have all the responsibility. Sole-parents can follow all the advice in *Good to Go* without modification.

Co-parents, on the other hand, both contribute resources and divide responsibilities. In the best-case scenario, co-parents work together to share decision-making and consult each other on parenting approaches.

However, if you exist in a high-conflict parenting dynamic, it can be difficult or impossible to "get on the same page." When it comes to potty training, this can pose an especially difficult and frustrating challenge.

Whenever possible, try to stick to common ground and discuss your child, not the method. It is completely out of your control whether you and your child's parent agree on potty training. What is in your control is how you spend the time you have with your child. You can make that time as impactful as possible by teaching them the *Good to Go* method and pick up where you left off when your child returns from a custody visit. Even if the other parent is doing something different, the goal is the same. Children are nothing if not flexible and adaptable. They can hold space for the way mommy does things versus daddy's method.

If and when you communicate with the other parent, focus on facts like "she used the potty three times today!" Don't try to persuade them to change their approach by saying "this is why my way is better."

Recently, I had a client, Emily, going through a super rough divorce that included having to move houses. Her life was already in tumult, and she suddenly needed to potty train her three-year-old daughter so she could attend a preschool close to her new house. Emily already felt like she had missed the potty-training window because of all the divorce drama and was feeling a lot of mom guilt as a result.

Emily harbored a lot of anger toward her ex-husband, Josh, because he was giving her almost no information at custody exchanges. They were required to communicate using a court-approved messaging app, and when Emily would try and share her approach to potty training, Josh would send curt responses like "okay" and "got it." She started to lose faith that he was even attempting to potty train and began to spiral that her daughter would be rejected from the new preschool for still being in diapers.

My suggestion was to completely stop asking how Josh was approaching potty training. Instead, she just needed to focus on her time with their daughter and trust the process. Although she never got a clear answer from Josh, she suspected he continued to put her in diapers, despite her clear request to try potty training.

But Emily's daughter was resilient. She continued to show good process, even though she spent half the time in diapers while with her dad. Emily noticed her daughter was identifying her body's cues and asking to go potty with more and more lead time, and was staying dry most days they were together.

Imagine Emily's surprise when her ex-husband messaged to brag that his daughter had used the big potty at his house! Her knee-jerk reaction was to roll her eyes and think, "Did he not even buy a floor potty?!" But, still, this was encouraging—it proved that Emily's daughter could maintain her progress, even in the face of these inconsistencies. It may have taken a little longer, but in the end, Emily's hands-off approach with her ex didn't add to their already-tense dynamic, and her daughter was able to go to school potty trained.

Grandparents (and Other Backseat Drivers)

By far, one of the most triggering things your child's grandparent can say is, "Oh, I potty trained you in one day! You're making this too complicated." Whether it's the softening effect of the passage of time (or maybe you *were* just the perfect child), it seems like your parents have forgotten how challenging it can be to have a toddler!

Generational differences in parenting can be a major challenge to navigate. Sometimes, it seems like we're doing nothing right in our parents' eyes. Potty training is a subject where people have strong opinions, and it can be hard for grandparents to bite their tongues when they see us attempting it differently. Just the other day, I heard a doozy from a parent named Stephen. Stephen said his mom was encouraging him to potty train his daughter the same way she potty trained him. How did she potty train him, you may wonder? She forced two-year-old Stephen to sit on the potty and wouldn't let him get up until he peed or pooped, no matter how long it took.

This is an extreme example, but there are many old-school approaches to potty training that just don't pass the vibe check with modern parents. These methods often rely on dominance and obedience, rather than *Good to Go*'s focus on body-awareness and cooperation.

Navigating these differences in approach can feel like walking through a minefield. It's a delicate balance between letting our parents know that we appreciated our upbringing but would like to attempt something different with our own children. (Or, perhaps, you didn't appreciate your upbringing, but don't want to hurt their feelings or start a fight.)

A grandparent with a lot of opinions can feel like a backseat driver: your hands are on the parenting wheel, but they're nagging you about where to turn and how fast to drive. But as the parent, you are the final authority on how you raise your child.

If the backseat driver is your partner's parent, try to let them do the talking. Unfortunately, some in-laws will only respect the word of their own kids and default to defensiveness and dismissiveness with their kid's spouse. If your partner can't or won't address the issue, the upside is that there's usually less emotional baggage involved with someone who wasn't directly responsible for raising you. Criticisms or suggestions about a different parenting style won't come off as ungrateful from an in-law because it wasn't their own childhood that's under scrutiny.

When you run into a conflict of opinion, in order to keep the peace, you'll benefit from finding some language that simultaneously acknowledges their contribution while also asserting your authority.

> "I know you have so much experience and wisdom from raising me, and I really value that. I hear your method worked well for you, but we are trying something different that I think will be a good fit for our kid. I'd love to tell you more about it."
>
> "You raised me with the best information you had at the time. More research has been done, and now we have more information, so we're trying a new approach."
>
> "This seems to be working out so far, and I'd love your support."

Stay focused on your common ground: your child! Both you and their grandparent want to support them in the best way possible, based on the information you have.

If you find the grandparent trying to subvert your authority by approaching potty training in a different way (say, setting up a rewards system without your permission), you will need to intervene. Talk adult-to-adult, without your child around, and explain that you would like to take the reins on potty training, and thank them for their concern. Then, without throwing their grandparent under the bus, explain to your child that there was just a difference in opinion. "Grandma was so excited to get started, she did it without me! But we'll be working on potty training together from now on."

Chapter in Review

- You are about to embark on a big journey with your child and it's okay to feel a bit overwhelmed. Prepare yourself emotionally as much as you can!
- Your involvement in potty training will go through phases: highly involved, occasionally involved, and rarely involved.
- Decide and commit to vocabulary for #1 and #2 with all caregivers. If they're already attending school, check to see what words their teachers use.
- If getting ready to welcome another baby, give yourself enough time to potty train before the baby arrives, or wait until you're past the newborn phase.
- Rule out any medical concerns.
- Get on the same page with your partner or other caregivers.
- If you are in a high-conflict co-parenting dynamic, stick to common ground (your child) and share resources (like this book!) if possible.
- Dealing with your own parents or in-laws can be tricky! Recognize and respect the generational differences while maintaining boundaries.

PART II

READY, SET, GO

5

Ready to Start

Hooray! You've loaded up your parenting-skills toolkit, assessed your child's developmental readiness, and now it's time to actually get started. But . . . how exactly do you do that?

Let's talk about the game plan. In this chapter, I'm going to teach you about something we're calling "the rehearsal period." This is a period of about two weeks where you're going to be intentionally practicing certain parts of going potty in a no-pressure, stress-free way. I'll be giving you a lot of specific, actionable advice on how to do this, so you'll be able to easily incorporate it into your daily life.

In the next chapter, "Set the Stage," we'll go over all the practical logistics for potty training: gear you'll need, books to read, and scripts to help prepare your kid. In Chapter 7, "It's Go Time," we'll get into all the nitty-gritty details of how to actually remove diapers and get your kid to use the potty. In Chapter 8, "Keep Going," we'll teach you exactly how to transition from the highly involved phase into the occasionally involved and rarely involved stages. Finally, in Chapter 9, "Expect the Unexpected" we'll address all kinds of potty-training issues and curveballs that may get thrown your way.

The Rehearsal Period

Have you ever heard of "the actor's nightmare"? It's a recurring dream performers have, where they're shoved on stage but don't know any of their lines. They're stuck in a play they haven't rehearsed, and the audience is staring at them, expecting them to act out a scene they've never practiced.

Sounds horrifying, right?

Now: imagine your toddler. They've spent their whole lives peeing and pooping in diapers. But one day they wake up and they're told the diapers are gone. Now it's time to use this weird bowl that makes loud, strange noises and you're supposed to do *what* in it? And their parents are looking at them, expecting they just know how to do it, and they just don't know what to do.

Unfortunately, this is what many potty-training methods do to kids. These quick-fix approaches expect kids to learn all the steps of using the potty at the same time. It's a sink-or-swim approach that's the equivalent of shoving an actor on stage and expecting them to learn their lines in front of a live audience.

We're not going to do that.

Instead, we're going to start with what we're calling "the rehearsal period," where your child gets to practice and learn while still in diapers. The rehearsal period lasts anywhere from two to four weeks.

Believe it or not, this is the most important part of the potty-training journey. You may think "potty training" doesn't start until you remove diapers, but this rehearsal period is actually where your child gets to do the most learning and will set them up for success when the first diaper-free day comes.

Wait, How Long Is This Going to Take?!

It may seem daunting to hear that you need at least two weeks to successfully complete the *Good to Go* method. After all, other popular potty-training methods promise success within a long weekend. You may be wondering why *Good to Go* differs on this, and that's a valid question!

The dirty (and very messy) secret is that the quick-fix methods often come with a lot of issues after the initial "training" period is complete. These methods don't take into account the spectrum of parental involvement and think kids are "done" once they've passed the high-involvement stage. But because these kids weren't given enough support before they went diaper free they get labeled as "potty trained" while they're still struggling with some of the basics.

Our goal is to front-load the learning before we take away diapers, that way the children can do most of their learning in a lower-stress (and lower-stakes) environment. By teaching our kids all the steps of going potty in a low-pressure yet structured way, they can practice and internalize them. This rehearsal period also gives children some time to get used to the new potty gear and emotionally prepare for the big change that's coming.

Pick a time at least two weeks from now where you can stay close to home for a few days while you start potty training. If you are traveling, changing schools, welcoming a new sibling, or have guests staying in your home, then it's best to wait. You can start practicing the techniques found in this chapter at any time, but you want to have at least two weeks to work on them. Don't start the rehearsal period more than four weeks before your official "potty-training" day, as the novelty tends to wear off and kids lose interest if you rehearse for too long.

VCP for Poop and Pee

In Chapter 2, "The Big Picture," you learned about my Values-Centered Parenting (VCP) tool. Now it's time to apply this framework to potty learning. Here's how we envision it for *Good to Go*:

1. *Identify the core value*: Body awareness
2. *Teach*: Prepare the environment, introduce the gear, connect sensation and action, describe intake and elimination, teach upskills*
3. *Model and narrate*: Narrate and mention your own potty use and awareness cues, announce your "routine tries"*
4. *Reinforce*: Notice and mention when they ask for a diaper change and when they attempt upskills

---

*These will be defined soon!

Teach
- Prepare the environment
- Introduce the gear
- Connect sensation & action
- Describe intake & elimination
- Teach Upskills*

Core Value: Body Awareness

Model
- Narrate your own awareness cues
- Announce your "Routine Tries"*

Reinforce
Notice and mention:
- When they ask for a diaper change
- When they attempt Upskills

We'll be going over all this in more detail, but for now I want us to remember that the *core values* we're aiming for are body awareness and potty independence. The big-picture goal is not clean floors, dry undies, or compliant children. By framing potty training with this VCP tool, we can keep this ultimate aim in mind and not sweat the small stuff.

The Universal Potty Sequence

I want to introduce you to something you already know by heart: how to use the toilet!

In order to go to the bathroom, we need to (1) Notice the sensation. (2) Navigate to a potty. (3) Pull down pants and/or underwear. (4) Sit on the potty. (5) Eliminate. (6) Wipe. (7) Flush. (8) Pull up underwear and/or pants. (9) Wash hands.

The Universal Potty Sequence

 **1.** Notice the sensation

 **2.** Navigate to a potty

 **3.** Pull down pants/undies

 **4.** Sit on potty

 **5.** Eliminate

 **6.** Wipe

 **7.** Flush

 **8.** Pull up pants/undies

 **9.** Wash hands

Obviously, for adults, this sequence is second nature and automatic. When we think of going to the bathroom, we think of it as one single action. But for young children, these nine distinct steps are all separate skills that must be learned and internalized.

Historically, potty training focused heavily on step 1, noticing the urge to go, and just assumed kids would pick up on steps 2–9 easily. But I believe we've been doing it backward.

In fact, the first step, feeling the sensation, is actually the last step to be mastered. As we learned in Chapter 3, "Rethinking Readiness," body awareness is complex and unique to each individual and requires trial and error to master. Because this is the most difficult thing to learn, it can be discouraging and disheartening for both kids and parents when it takes longer than expected.

We're going to flip the usual approach, and spend a few weeks in the rehearsal period, gently teaching steps 2–9 of the Universal Potty Sequence (UPS) before we remove diapers. This allows kids to master up to 90 percent of the process in a calm, respectful, and no-pressure way. They get to experience confidence and mastery around pottying before they've even officially started. Then, when it's time to remove diapers, they're only learning one new skill, instead of nine. This helps reduce overwhelm and stress, not to mention messes and meltdowns.

So, how do we practice these skills without actually potty training? We're going to use the magic of upskilling.

Upskilling the Universal Potty Sequence

The main work of the rehearsal period is going to be upskilling your child in steps 2–9 of the UPS before you start removing diapers.

Upskilling the UPS

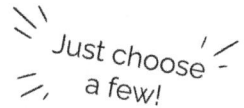 *Just choose a few!*

 1. No upskill needed - they will learn this later!

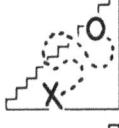 2. Change diapers in bathroom

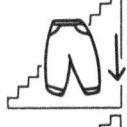 3. Practice pulling down pants

 4. Climb + balance on potty

 5. Dispose of diaper contents into toilet

 6. Practice a final wipe

 7. Flush on their own

 8. Pull up pants/undies

 9. Always wash hands!

Here's a breakdown of how you could apply upskills to each step:

1. *Notice the sensation.*
   This is the only step where upskilling isn't applicable. Don't worry, we go over how to handle this when you begin potty training!

2. *Navigate to a potty.*
   An easy upskill is to move all diaper changes to the bathroom. This helps your child associate bathroom activities with where "potty stuff" happens. When your child has a full diaper, lead them to the bathroom for the change. For wet diapers, you can do a quick stand-up change, and for poopy ones, you can lay them down on the bathroom floor.

3. *Pull down pants and/or underwear.*
   Have your child help pull down their pants or lift up their skirt before each diaper change. This is best done in front of a full-length mirror so they can watch themselves. This small step is actually an essential skill because, as we all know, when you really need to go, every second counts! Getting them used to this process helps build independence (and muscle memory) and ensures they're ready to manage their clothes quickly when it's time to use the potty. It's a simple habit that will make a big difference when you move to full potty training.

4. *Sit on the potty.*
   Practice the choreography! Climbing up the stool, turning around, and balancing on the potty takes a lot of coordination. Or, if using a floor potty, your child still has to learn how to land on that seat without slipping off. You can practice these things during neutral times between diaper changes so it's fun and lighthearted.

5. *Eliminate.*
   You can practice peeing or pooping after a diaper change, especially if you're already in the bathroom. Once they are out

of their diaper you can see if they have any interest in sitting to see if there are "any drops left?" Make sure there is no pressure to actually go; it is just offering them an opportunity and getting them used to the sequence of events.

6. *Wipe.*
   This is, by far, one of the hardest skills to build and it actually takes years to master, but you can start small. After a diaper change, if it was just a pee, hand them some toilet paper and let them try to clean themselves. If this was a poopy diaper then get most of it cleaned up before you let them try!

7. *Flush.*
   This is the golden ticket! It's possible your kid is already doing this, because toddlers cannot resist being in charge of flushing the toilet. And once your child gets the chance to flush their own waste they will be hooked. Especially that first poop! You can start by taking poopy diapers and rolling the waste into the toilet and inviting your toddler to flush. If your kid is so enthusiastic about this process that it must happen after every diaper change, even the pee-only ones, you can take the diaper and pretend to squeeze a few drops into the toilet so it can be flushed.

8. *Pull up underwear and/or pants.*
   This is the same as step 3, just in reverse. It may be interesting to note which step is easier for your child, and whether there's any obstacles (like buttons or zippers) that get in their way. This is a great time to assess clothing choices going forward— you may want to put away the denim overalls or full-body jumpsuits for a time.

9. *Wash hands.*
   While your children already know how to wash their hands, you can start building independence by asking them to turn on the water themselves, pump the soap onto their hands, turn off the water, and dry their hands after.

Keep in mind, these are all just options. I wouldn't recommend upskilling all of these steps at the same time, or doing every upskill at every diaper change. Instead, you can pick a handful of skills to focus on and pepper them in here and there over the course of the rehearsal period. Follow your child's interest and make it fun and playful.

The only exception is for step 9, *wash hands*—this step should ALWAYS be done after a diaper change, even if it's inconvenient. Not only is hand washing crucial for health and safety, but it's a frequent cause of power struggles between parents and kids. If you start enforcing mandatory hand washing early on, this will hopefully curb resistance when they actually start using the potty and it's more mission critical.

> ### BUBBLE GLOVES!
>
> My favorite trick for teaching kids how to soap up their hands is to say "make bubble gloves!" Little kids love this metaphor, and it's a clear visual to help them understand that soap needs to get between each finger.

Modeling Meets Narration

As someone reading a parenting book, you're likely already familiar with the concept of modeling. The idea that children learn behaviors, attitudes, and values by observing and imitating their parents is not groundbreaking. But it's often sold to us as the solution to all our parenting challenges: by demonstrating desired behaviors consistently, parents can effectively teach their children.

But there's a major piece that's missing from the conversation around modeling: how crucial it is to pair it with *narration*. Yes, it's important for parents to model behavior for their kids, but if the actions aren't paired with communication, kids aren't going to learn what's going on inside your body and mind.

Here's an example: let's say you're struggling to stay hydrated and want to teach your child to drink enough water. If we're focused on modeling alone, you'd just drink more water in front of them. Maybe you'd get a new reusable water bottle and refill it multiple times a day. But while a child would observe you drinking more water, they're really only getting about 20 percent of the lesson just by watching alone.

Because what's actually going on internally? How did you know you were thirsty? What sensations were you feeling that cued you in to the need to refill your water bottle? You may be processing all these feelings, but all of this was invisible to your child!

This is where narration comes in. Instead of keeping it all inside, it's important to tell your child the internal process you're going through, so they can start to create those skills. It may sound something like this:

"Hmmm, my mouth is feeling so dry! It's like a desert in there! And, now that I think about it, my throat is a little rough feeling, and I'm not as energetic as I should be. I feel sluggish! And my head hurts a little. Hmmm, these are all clues that I'm dehydrated—I'm really thirsty and I didn't even notice! I'm going to fill up my water bottle and see if that helps me feel better."

With narration, you're granting access to your internal processing and allowing your child to connect with their own internal cues as well. This skill is crucial when it comes to potty learning.

Modeling and Narration during the Rehearsal Period

While we're using upskilling to practice steps 2–9 of the UPS, modeling and narration is how we're going to practice step 1, recognizing their body's cues.

If your kid ever joins you in the bathroom, you're already doing the modeling part. Never going to the bathroom alone is one of the most common parenting gripes, but I'm here to reframe it: you've just been modeling good toilet habits all along! And even if you somehow manage to get privacy from a toddler (please, tell me your secrets!), they have still observed you needing to take periodic breaks.

What I'd like you to add in now is the *narration* part. Whenever you feel the urge to go to the bathroom, start talking about it.

> "Wow, I'm feeling some pressure down there. I think it may be time for me to poop! I'm going to go try and see if anything comes out."
>
> "Hmm, I feel a little tickle low in my pelvis. That usually means I have to pee. I'm going to go right now!"

By really getting specific and clear about what's going on in your body, you're going to help your child begin to connect their body cues with the need to go.

In addition to modeling and narrating your own body cues, you can start adding in narration about your observations of their body as it relates to potty training. Things like "Wow, is your diaper wet? Does it feel heavy?" or "It looks like you're pushing out some poop! How does that feel? Difficult or easy?"

The Routine Try

While it's all the rage to listen to your body's cues, there are times when we go to the bathroom regardless of how we feel. This is the "just in case" stop to make sure our bladders are empty.

Some examples include:

- First thing in the morning
- Right before bedtime
- Before stepping into a bath or shower
- Before leaving the house
- Before walking into a movie theater
- When you stop for gas during a long car trip

I call this a "routine try" because it's an attempt we make based not on our body's cues, but on an element of our daily routines, or based on predictable experiences. (We may not go to a movie every day, but we all know it's routine to pee before you enter the theater so you don't miss an important scene.)

As adults, these bathroom breaks are just built into our routines, and we don't think much about them. You probably don't have to force yourself to pee first thing in the morning, it just happens automatically.

This is not the case with kids. In fact, these routine tries are a very common cause of power struggles between children and their caregivers. You may even remember your parents begging you to "just TRY before we leave, please!" (Or you may remember your parents' exasperation as they pulled over to a gas station five minutes into your road trip.)

My hope is that you preempt this power struggle by normalizing routine tries during this potty-training rehearsal period. We're trying to embed routine tries into your child's understanding of what it is to be a human who uses a toilet—everyone does it, so it's no big deal.

To do this, there's two main steps:

1. Model and narrate your own routine tries.
2. Come up with a family term for routine tries.

The first step is pretty straightforward, the most challenging part is to remember to do it! As I mentioned above, you probably don't even think twice about your routine tries, so you'll have to do a little extra work to notice when you're about to attempt one and then model and narrate it for your child.

The second step will require a little creativity. While "routine try" is an accurate description of this phenomenon, I must admit that it lacks pizzazz. Kids aren't going to jump to attention at the prospect of this clinically dry phrase.

Instead, I recommend coming up with a fun term that will appeal to your child, specifically. These could be real phrases or even just funny nonsense words. Some ideas:

- Pit stop
- Potty pop-in

- Zoom stop
- Wizzle wazzle
- Flush-a-doo
- Tinkle toot

You could even ask your kid to come up with the phrase after they've witnessed you doing a routine try. Making difficult situations fun and silly can be a parent's best tool. And having a "secret code" in your family can be a great way to make your kid feel like you're all on the same team.

Whatever you decide on, this phrase will act as a shorthand for the lengthy explanation of why they have to go to the bathroom, even if they don't feel like going. After all, which prompt sounds more like one a young child will agree to?

"Lucas, you need to do a routine try before going to the park! It's important to empty our bladders, even if we don't feel the sensation. Let's go potty."

"Lucas, it's time for a squiggle-dee-boop!"

I think we all know the answer! Kids like brevity and silliness—this is a no-brainer.

And imagine your child's giggles when you model and narrate, "Wow, we're about to leave the house! I better go do my squiggle-dee-boop!"

This term for a routine try will be doing heavy lifting on day one of potty training. On that first day, you'll be prompting them a lot, so it's good to get this concept well established during the rehearsal period.

What's Your Pooping Posture?

Here's a question I bet nobody has ever asked you before: What does your child's posture look like when they're pooping? Are they squatting? Standing? Leaning over a table, maybe?

If you don't know, I'd encourage you to observe how your kid naturally poops *before* you remove diapers. If you're about to start potty training, it's likely you can more or less predict the timing of their poops. They may be hiding or asking for privacy, but I'd like you to discreetly take a peek and see how they're positioned while pooping.

I've started asking this question in my parenting classes, and almost half of the parents report that their kids are either standing or leaning to poop in a diaper.

Now, how do *you* poop? I'm going to guess that 50 percent of you aren't pooping while standing. In fact, adults consistently either sit or squat to poop—this is true across cultures and even in places where toilets aren't available. Squatting with your knees above your hips is actually the ideal pooping posture, physiologically—there's even a whole category of step-stool products designed to get you into a squatting position while on the toilet.

Now, here's one more embarrassing thought experiment: imagine trying to poop while standing upright. What muscles would you engage to push the stool out? Can you even activate those muscles as an adult who has been squatting to poop for so long? I know I can't! In fact, we've developed our core muscles to avoid that from ever happening in the first place.

If your child currently stands or leans over while pooping, their pelvic floor muscles are working differently than yours. They have somehow managed to figure out a way to coordinate their muscles to poop in a completely different position. Which is, honestly, pretty impressive—bodies are cool! But if this is the case, what's going to happen if you suddenly take away their diapers and ask them to poop on a potty? It's going to feel just as unnatural as if I asked you to start pooping while standing up.

The rehearsal period is the best time to start guiding your child into a squatting position for poops. If we build up their pelvic floor muscles and coordination while they're still wearing diapers, it lessens the stress and pressure on kids when they start using a potty instead. I can't tell you how many families tell me their kid has mastered peeing on the potty, but refuses to poop on the potty. So many of these withholding issues could be prevented just by fixing their pooping posture before removing diapers.

So, how do we get your kid to do this? Here are a few approaches you can take to help get them into the right posture:

If you can catch them in the act (or just before):

- Stand face-to-face with your child and hold their hands, begin to squat yourself (modeling!) while gently guiding them into a squatting position. Warning: this is an effective approach that many toddlers straight-up reject. Don't be worried if your kid won't cooperate or thinks you're weird for trying this, and just move on to other methods!

- Strike a pose!: if they're into animals, ask them to show you what a frog looks like. If they like superheroes, maybe they can crouch like they're about to pounce on a bad guy.

- Wall wiggles: have them stand with their back against the wall and ask them to slide all the way down to the floor.

- Self-reflection: take your phone or tablet and open up your front-facing camera and place it on the floor. Many toddlers will crouch down just to get a better look at themselves!

- Screen-time bribery: placing an enticing video game on a tablet or phone on the floor may encourage a toddler to crouch down to interact with it.

Build their muscles at neutral times. These should all be practiced while already in a squatting position, but not while they're actively pooping:

- Blowing bubbles: grab a bubble wand and encourage your kid to blow bubbles. This helps activate core muscles while also relaxing the anal sphincter muscles.

- Trumpeting: pretend you're elephants and make trumpeting sounds.

- Grunt it out: make loud grunting noises like a rhinoceros

- Fart it out: ask your kid if they can squeeze out a fart. Most toddlers think farting is hilarious, so this should be fun for them.

For bonus points, practice these while sitting on the potty, fully clothed. This helps your child connect the feeling with the venue, without the pressure of actually pooping.

The Subtle Art of Wiping Your Own Butt

You may want to sit down before you read this. Are you ready?
You're probably going to be wiping your kid's butt until they're five (maybe longer).
I know, I know, this isn't the news you want to hear! After all, so much of the discourse around potty training is, "well, at least you won't be wiping butts anymore!"
Unfortunately, wiping is the hardest part of the potty-training process to teach effectively. Even though we include wiping in the Universal Potty Sequence, and encourage you to upskill your child in this step during the rehearsal period, this is not a skill they will be able to master right away.
This is mostly because so much of wiping relies on non-teachable skills. First, kids must develop the coordination and balance to reach around and wipe. They have to have the maturity to understand why it's important to have a clean behind. And they also need the observation skills to know when they're done wiping.
At an even more fundamental level, kids just need to grow big enough to reach their own butts. Children's bodily proportions are significantly different than an adult's. To demonstrate this, ask your child to put their arms around their head, like they're diving into a pool. Notice how their arms hug their head tightly, and their hands struggle to meet in the middle. Now, you try it: your arms are way above your head!

Artists often use head height to mark out proportions in a figure drawing. It's a shortcut to help draw accurate representations of people, and it can help us understand this difference. Adults are about 7.5 heads high; toddlers are 3.5 heads high. That means, while an adult's head is about 13 percent of their height, a toddler's head is nearly 30 percent of their total stature.

So, when it comes to wiping, your toddler may be physically incapable of easily reaching around their own body. It may require some fancy bending techniques for them to get the right angle.

That said, you may *need* to teach your kid to wipe before they're ready. Depending on their licensing, preschools may not legally be allowed to assist in wiping (or toileting at all). Many public schools have introduced universal pre-kindergarten for four-year-olds, which has the same licensing issue where teachers are barred from helping with anything in the bathroom.

To teach your kid to at least attempt a wipe, you should start while clothed. Practicing at non-potty times can lower the pressure and allow your child to make mistakes without also making a mess.

Step 1: Scrunch or Fold?

How do you hold toilet paper when you wipe yourself? Now ask some of your closest friends (maybe some other potty-training parents, so they won't judge you)—you may be surprised at how much your styles differ!

You probably never think about how you hold your toilet paper, but this is a specific skill we need to teach our kids! Remember, they need to learn everything from the ground up, from how much toilet paper to pull off the roll to how to hold it.

From my research, the two main ways people hold their toilet paper are in a *scrunch* or a *fold*. The scrunch is basically just wadding up a length of toilet paper, which gives you a lot of surface area and cushion. Proponents of the scrunch claim it protects your hand better and is more absorbent. The fold is more organized, where the toilet paper is laid end over end in a tidy pile, and allows you to re-fold for a second wipe. Fold enthusiasts claim it's the more civilized approach and gives you a better visual of whether you've wiped properly.

Whichever method you teach your child, make sure you also teach them how much toilet paper to pull off the roll. This will also vary by family, but almost every kid is going to try to pull way too much toilet paper off at the beginning! Keep in mind that young kids will likely require a few passes, so pick an amount that won't clog your toilet with multiple tries. If you have a wall-mounted toilet-paper holder, you could even put a piece of painter's tape on the wall to mark the desired length of toilet paper.

LAURA'S CONFESSION

When Gia and I were in the final push to write this book, we decided to take a writer's retreat out to Palm Desert. There, instead of getting a massage or swimming in the pool, we spent three straight days holed up in our hotel rooms writing about poop and pee.

Maybe we started to get a little stir crazy, or maybe all this potty talk was going to our heads, but we started getting a little silly. At some point, Gia took a bathroom break and returned to ask me a question I wasn't expecting, "Laura, what are you: a scruncher or a folder?"

I looked at her, confused. It took me a second to realize she was talking about my toilet paper technique.

"Actually, I'm a wrapper."

I may well have said I was born on Nepture. Gia's jaw dropped to the floor, and she said, "What the heck do you mean? How???"

I then spent the next five minutes explaining that I wrap the toilet paper 360 degrees around my hand. That way I get all the benefits of the fold, but with extra protection.

This is how my mom taught me, and I honestly didn't know there was another way! And you better believe I'm teaching my boys to be wrappers, too!

Step 2: Find a Wiping Position

While your child is in clothes, you can try a couple of different tactics for wiping. Once they've loaded up the toilet paper, you can try these options:

- Stand up, with legs separated. Place their non-dominant hand on the ground, creating a stable tripod. With their other hand, reach through the gap in their legs to wipe their bottom.
- While sitting on the potty, have them twist their torso around and attempt to hook their hand underneath their backside. See if they can reach around and pull up to wipe.
- While sitting on the potty, have them reach between their legs and push.

No matter which technique you try, emphasize the importance of wiping front to back.

This is especially important for children with vulvas, as fecal bacteria can cause vaginal infections and urinary tract infections.

Another great time to practice their wiping position is in the bath or shower! This is a low-stakes, mess-free way to rehearse the mechanics of wiping. Just make sure it's not too slippery before they move their body into a wiping position. They can use a washcloth to mimic toilet paper, and have them practice the front-to-back wiping motion.

You'll also want to teach them to look at the toilet paper and see if there's any brown spots on it. If they see poop, they need to fold the toilet paper and wipe again! Teach them to wipe until they don't see any brown streaks any more, and get more toilet paper if needed.

You may have seen a viral video of a preschool teacher teaching her students how to wipe. She had tied two balloons together and affixed them to the back of a toddler chair, and then used them to represent butt cheeks as she demonstrated wiping with toilet paper. While this video was truly adorable, I have no idea if it's effective. This may be a good way for a child to understand the basic mechanics of getting between the cheeks, but I'm skeptical about how useful it is beyond that. This balloon trick won't replace actual wiping practice with their own bodies, but if you're looking for a cute activity, it wouldn't hurt to try.

As mentioned, better place to practice "wiping without wiping" would be in the bathtub. You can hand your child their washcloth and ask them to wash between their butt cheeks. See how they naturally try to reach it, and then give them some instructions about how to do it if they struggle. One warning: I would avoid the standing technique here because it could be slippery and dangerous!

Step 3: Wash Your Hands!

Even though you're not actually wiping a poopy butt during these practice sessions, I still want you to teach your child the closing steps after wiping. This means: dropping the toilet paper in the toilet, flushing, and then washing your hands thoroughly with soap and water.

Many kids are resistant to hand washing, and this is a situation where it's not negotiable. You can explain how poop can make you sick and washing hands can prevent future throw ups or pink eye. There's a fine line between inspiring good hygiene and creating a paranoid germaphobe, so you're going to need to feel this one out for yourself. Whatever your approach, the bottom line is that kids know there's no leaving the bathroom without washing their hands.

Fading Involvement

Wiping is another situation where our concept of "scaffolding" comes into play. At first, you'll likely be highly involved with wiping, probably even holding your hand over theirs as they wipe.

Later, you can be in the bathroom to observe their first attempts and then provide any final wipes that are necessary to get them completely clean.

By the time your child starts at a school where they can't assist with wiping, you will want them to be as proficient as possible.

Not the Model, Still the Teacher

When a parent has a baby with different genitals from their own, there's often blind spots that come to light. Many dads are blindsided by the importance of wiping front to back with their baby girls, as nobody ever bothered to teach them about this.

You may be in a family where your children have different genitals than their parents. I have worked with a number of two-mom families with only male children and two-dad families with only daughters. Also, we know many children are growing up with single parents, so there will not always be an adult around with the same genitals.

Though we put a lot of emphasis on modeling during the learning process, it's not necessary for a parent's genitals to match their child's for it to be effective. The only problem comes when there is a skill that a parent may not have direct experience with and may not know the correct way to teach. For instance, when my sons started standing up to pee, I legitimately didn't know if they needed to wipe or not. As a woman, we wipe every time we go, but do men?

If you have a trusted friend or family member who matches your child's anatomy, ask them if they'd be willing to answer your awkward, potty-related questions for you. And while the internet can be a bit of a minefield, there are actually entire forums where people debate these kinds of questions. Wherever you get your information, be reassured that your child doesn't need you to have matching genitalia in order to learn to potty!

MAMA, WHERE'S YOUR PENIS?

During potty training, I was diligent about modeling and narrating my own potty habits. I was also dedicated to teaching my boys the proper names for their anatomy and making sure they understood exactly how their bodies worked.

> Before he turned three, Sebastian was able to correctly identify his penis and explain to any passing stranger how "I dwink fwom my water bottle and it turn into pee!"
>
> One morning, after he had rudely woken me up at 5:30 a.m., I groggily carried him into the bathroom so we could both attempt our first routine try of the morning. He sat and peed, and said "wow, so much pee coming out of my penis!" It was too early for me to do much more than to unenthusiastically say, "yeah, wow. My turn."
>
> We switched places and I sat down to use the toilet. As he heard me urinate, he said "wow, mama, so much pee coming out of YOUR penis!"
>
> "I don't have a penis," I told him.
>
> His jaw dropped. "WHAT? Mama, where's your penis? Where it go?!?"
>
> The poor child thought mine had fallen off.
>
> We then had a whole discussion about anatomy and how we both have urethras, but his goes through his penis while mine is in my vulva. I honestly didn't think I'd start my day Googling "toddler-friendly genital anatomy" before the sun came up, but having children is a constant adventure into the unknown.

Now that you understand upskilling, modeling and narration, and pooping posture, you'll spend the next two-ish weeks working on these things with your child. In the meantime, you can also start preparing your home and life for the logistics of removing diapers. In the next chapter, we'll discuss all the gear and strategies you'll need.

Chapter in Review

- The rehearsal period should last between two and four weeks.
- To plan the rehearsal period, find a date when you can stay close to home for a few days to dedicate to potty training and

work backward. Avoid starting during travel, school changes, or other major events.

- Introduce the 9-step UPS, something you are already very familiar with but your child may find novel.
- Step 1 (feel the sensation) is the last thing kids master, so focus on steps 2–9 instead.
- Choose a few upskills from steps 2–9 to focus on, rather than trying to do them all at once.
- Modeling when you use the potty is not enough. Start to narrate how you know that you need to go. Describe the sensations in your body and say them out loud for your child to hear.
- You will also need to model when you don't feel the urge to go, but try anyway. We call this the routine try. For example: before getting in the car, right before bed, and so on.
- Prevent future pooping problems and power struggles with observing how your child poops while still in diapers, and fix their pooping posture if needed.

6

Set the Stage

In the previous chapter, we discussed the big-picture approaches for the rehearsal period. In this chapter, we're going to get into the logistical details. You've got the theory down, now you need a shopping list and some specific action items.

Separate Daytime and Sleeping Diapers

As discussed in previous chapters, we are not going to address (or worry about) nighttime dryness at all during the initial potty-training process. But, in a few weeks, after the rehearsal period, you'll be taking away diapers during waking hours only. This can be confusing and difficult to explain to a toddler—after all, we hype up the toilet learning process and then stick them in a diaper just a few hours later for their first nap?

The way to avoid this confusion is to establish a *clear and visible* difference between their daytime and nighttime diapers now. You can do this by buying diapers with different colors, patterns, or characters depending on the time of day. For instance, your daytime diapers may be plain white pull-ups, and your nighttime diapers are blue tabbed diapers with their favorite Sesame Street Muppet on them. Or, if you want to work through your existing stash, you could take a permanent marker and draw a sun on the daytime diapers and a moon and stars on the ones used at night.

The specifics are not so important as long as they're visually distinct. And, of course, you're going to have to narrate this for your child. Tell them all about how there's now "daytime diapers" and "nighttime diapers" and show them how to tell the difference. Start identifying which type you're putting on during diaper changes: "It's bedtime, so I'm putting on a nighttime diaper now! See how it has a moon on it? That's how you know!"

You may also need to create a third category: "school diapers." If your child attends a preschool that has a potty-training policy that will continue to place them in diapers (for instance, if there's a certain number of misses, or they just won't remove diapers until the kid is fully potty trained), you may work with their teachers to establish "school diapers" as distinct from "home daytime diapers."

The goal of all this is to ease the transition into the sleep-only diapering that will happen once you officially begin potty training. Your child won't be confused because they already understand that daytime and nighttime diapers are distinctly different objects.

Curate Their Wardrobe

Dressing kids in cute clothes is one of the major benefits of parenthood. There's nothing more adorable than a stylish toddler.

Unfortunately, now is not the time for high fashion. And I'm not just talking about the messes that come with potty training. Obviously, you don't want to risk soiling fancy clothes with a miss—sequins, feathers, and dry-clean only items are not going to last long during potty training.

What I'm more concerned about is your child's ability to quickly and easily use the potty. If you've ever needed to use a portable toilet at a music festival while wearing a romper, you may understand this plight. While overalls are truly the cutest, they're nearly impossible for small kids to figure out on their own. Same goes for pants with buttons, or tight leggings.

In the lead-up to potty training, we're going to be upskilling pulling down their own clothing so they can go potty. Let's set them up for success by giving them dresses and loose pants with elastic waistbands.

One more thing to consider: their bottoms are going to be smaller without diapers on! This may mean you'll have to go a size down in pants, lest they fall down their suddenly smaller behinds. If you aren't sure, do a try-on practice right after you've removed a wet diaper, before you fully change them, and have them run around and see if the pants stay up!

A BOY MOM'S BLIND SPOT

My older son, Auggie, has always been very gender conforming. His spontaneous love for cars, trucks, and superheroes was undeniable from a very young age. As such, his entire wardrobe is full of very masculine styles, with nary a skirt nor sequin in sight.

Sebastian, being the younger brother, has mostly been clothed in Auggie's hand-me-downs. And he's usually happy with them, as he shares Auggie's deep love of construction machinery and martial arts. So, when we started potty training, I dressed Sebastian in mostly loose, cotton pants. He did all his upskilling and toilet practice either naked, in shorts, or in pants, and I didn't think twice about it.

This wasn't an issue until recently, when Sebastian became enamored with a Disney princess dress he found at Target. He spotted the ice-blue, puffy Elsa dress as we were wheeling through the clothing racks, and it has now become his favorite piece of clothing. If it makes him happy, it makes me happy.

But the first time he wore it, we almost had a potty disaster. I realized I had never taught him how to bunch up the skirt and hold it around his waist. He pulled it up a little, but most of the skirt ended up underneath him as he sat on the small floor potty. Thankfully, I caught him before he pooped, and showed him how to gather up the fabric and keep it out of the way. It was a close call, but the Frozen dress lived to see another day.

(That said, "let it go" is an excellent song to encourage a kid to release on the potty, so keep that in your back pocket.)

Get the Gear

Potty training comes with some specialized equipment. The main categories of new gear you'll need are:

- Floor potties
- Toilet seat attachments
- Potty accessories

While the specifics of which items you buy will vary between each family, I recommend you have at least one item from each category to start with. Let's go over what there is to offer.

Floor Potties

These are small potty-training toilets that can be used in any room. They will have a small, often-removable receptacle that catches pee and poop so you can go dump it in your actual toilet afterward.

If you are repulsed by the idea of this kind of potty, you're not alone. Many parents ask if they can skip this item and just have their kid go straight to the big potty. And, it's possible that you may have a kid who does okay with only using the actual toilet from day one. But the vast majority of toilet learners don't have the ability to hold their pee long enough to get to the bathroom, at least not at the beginning. In fact, most families benefit from having a few of these floor potties so they can always be at the ready. (Plus, you'll be surprised at how normal it becomes to walk across your house with a bucket full of pee. Sorry!)

There are seemingly a hundred different styles of these floor potties, all promising to be the best option. Here are some features to take into consideration, along with some brand recommendations.

Seat Height

Floor potties vary in height quite a bit. Some are built for larger kids, like the Munchkin Arm & Hammer Multi-Stage 3-in-1 Potty Chair, while others are good for children on the smaller side, like the IKEA

Lilla. Ideally, you want your child's knees to be above their hips when sitting on the potty. (If you can't achieve this, you can use some yoga blocks or books to help raise their feet.)

Splash Guard

Most floor potties will have a little raised section in the front of the seat. This acts as a splash guard to catch pee. A higher guard is helpful if your kid has a penis and sits to pee (more on that decision later). The OKBaby Pasha and the Contours Bravo models have some of the largest splash guards I've found.

Comfort

Though it's not necessarily a requirement, considering your child's comfort while sitting may help encourage them to sit on the potty! This is especially true if your child has sensory sensitivities and may not like the feeling of a backless potty chair or a hard plastic seat. The BabyBjörn Potty Chair has a high backrest, while the Regalo 2-in-1 chair has a removable cushioned seat.

Novelty Features

All functionality aside, having a playful potty can be really fun for your child! You could get something like the Summer Infant My Size Potty Pro, which is shaped just like a real toilet, complete with pretend flushing noises. Or you could get a potty that plays songs or music, like the Baby Einstein Geared for Success 2-in-1 Potty Training System (this one also has a "character-revealing pot" that displays a cute cartoon frog when it gets wet). There's also many potties on the market that are branded with your kid's favorite characters.

Transition Features

Many potties are multi-purpose and will grow with your child. If you're tight on space, these can be a great option. For example, the Munchkin Arm & Hammer Multi-Stage 3-in-1 Potty Chair has a removable seat that doubles as a toilet seat insert, and the potty can be used as a step stool when the lid is closed.

Toilet Seat Attachments

Adult-sized toilet seats are way too big for little toddler butts. They will fall right through if they sit on them without assistance. This can be a major source of fear and anxiety for many potty-training children, so we want to make sure they feel physically safe and supported when they choose to use the big potty.

There are three main types of toilet seat attachments: permanent, fold-down seats that you install to replace your current toilet seat; removable inserts; and step-stool seats.

Permanent Seat Attachments

These toilet seats are truly ingenious. They are just like a normal toilet seat, with an adult-sized ring and a lid on a hinge, but they add a fold-down, kid-sized ring in between the adult's seat and the lid. The NextStep2 Potty Training Seat even has a magnet that keeps the kid's seat from falling down when an adult is using the toilet.

These can be found at most hardware stores or ordered online and are easily installed, often with just a wrench. I would recommend installing these on all toilets your child may use, as they're the most convenient and space-saving option and will be useful for years to come.

Removable Inserts

You can get inserts that run the gamut from incredibly minimalist to elaborate. The Jool Baby Folding Travel Potty Training Seat is flat and no-frills, but it folds down into a small pouch. Or you could get the Angelbliss Baby Potty Training Toilet Seat, which is very contoured and has a cushioned seat and handles for your child to hold on to.

It can be awkward to find a place to store these potty seats when they're not in use, and be sure to check the sizing of your toilet seat—if these are unstable in the bowl, your child may slip.

Step-Stool Seats

This product combines a step stool and a potty-seat insert. If you have a spare bathroom that only your child will be using, you may consider getting one of these attachments. These tend to be quite bulky, but also quite sturdy, and may give a nervous child a better sense of safety while perched on the potty. Sometimes called "potty-training ladders," a popular folding version is made by Jool Baby.

Potty Accessories

There's a few more items I'm going to recommend. Some of them are logical, like having wipes around, and others may be unexpected.

Step Stools

Step stools are a necessary but often-overlooked piece of potty-training gear. A step stool isn't just for climbing onto the toilet—it's actually doing double duty. Not only does it help your child feel safe and balanced while on the seat, but it also gets their body into a better position for pooping.

As an adult, you may have used a special footstool (like the Squatty Potty) to get into an optimal position for going poop, and kids need the same kind of support! There's two reasons why this position is ideal from a physiological standpoint. First, having knees above hips allows your child's muscles to relax, making it easier to poop. Second, having their feet firmly planted on something stable is crucial—if their legs dangle, they won't have any resistance to help push out the poop. It's important to make sure the step stool is tall enough to achieve this position, so you may need a two-step stool to get to the right height, especially if your child has shorter legs. (For more on this, see "What's Your Pooping Posture?" in Chapter 5, "Ready to Start.")

Even if you're exclusively using a floor potty, it's best to have a step stool at your bathroom sink to facilitate independent hand washing. If space is at a premium, there are many clever collapsible stools on the market that fold flat.

Non-Flushable Wet Wipes

While your child is learning, they may not want to use dry toilet paper. Also, potty training is messy, and wet wipes are useful for wiping butts as well as small messes on the floor. Having a pack of wipes right next to each potential potty-training station (floor potties or bathrooms) will just make your life easier.

I used to recommend flushable wipes for the bathroom, but there's increasing evidence that these are terrible for pipes, septic systems, and the environment. So now I recommend sticking with non-flushable, disposable baby wipes, and just make sure you have a good trash can.

Small Trash Can with a Lid

Since you're going to be using non-flushable wipes, make sure you have a bathroom trash can with a lid. This will help keep odors down and minimize visual mess.

Dressing Chair

Having a small, child-sized chair in the bathroom can be very useful to assist kids with dressing and undressing for the potty. Young children don't often have the coordination to stand on one leg to remove pants and having a chair in the bathroom can help them change clothes without having to sit on the floor.

Books and Toys

You can put some quiet toys and books in a basket by the toilet. This is not just for entertainment when going #2—comforting toys or engaging books can help a child relax enough to release a poop.

A Full Change of Clothes

Place a complete set of clothes in the bathroom so a child can change quickly and discreetly after a miss. If your child is sensitive or shy, this can help save them from the possible embarrassment of needing to leave the bathroom naked or wait alone for you to return with a new outfit. You can also stash extra clothes in the playroom or wherever you hang out during the day.

Travel Gear

When you're on the go, it's helpful to have some potty gear on hand. Public restrooms present a myriad of challenges for potty-training children and having some alternatives available can make everyone's lives easier. (We'll discuss public bathrooms in depth in the Chapter 8, "Keep Going.")

To keep it simple, you could just put a floor potty in the trunk of your car, along with wipes and extra clothes. You can line the floor potty with a plastic bag and a diaper, or a puppy pad.

A more convenient option is to buy a dedicated travel potty. A popular version is the OXO Tot 2-in-1 Go Potty. This item comes with plastic liners that have an absorbent pad inside, for easy cleanup. It stores flat, but has legs that fold down to make a little potty stand, or you can fold it outward and use it as a seat insert.

Another useful item to have on hand is a travel urinal. These work for boys and girls, and are obviously only for pee emergencies. But if you're out and about and your kid has to pee right away, they can be a quicker solution than setting up a travel potty or finding a bathroom. You can find reusable ones with cute designs, or disposable urinal bags with absorbent gel inside and zipper tops. The disposable ones fold into little packets and can be easily thrown into a purse or diaper bag.

Do I Really Need All This Stuff?

Our world is built for able-bodied adults. Children spend their entire days navigating environments that aren't made for them—they have to be picked up to use public bathroom sinks, require step stools to reach countertops, and need a boost to climb into cars. Because this is the status quo, most people don't think about it. But it's a constant obstacle for our kids and requires them to put in so much effort just to complete their daily tasks.

Instead of thinking of all this potty gear as extra junk, bound to clutter up your house and empty your wallet, I'd like you to reframe it as *accessibility gear* for your child. Do you absolutely *need* a floor potty in every room? Maybe not. But will having a floor potty nearby help your child be more independent and confident in this process? Absolutely.

And while this is a huge laundry list of items, you won't need all of it. You need to take into account your living space, your child's temperament, and your budget. The good news is that it's often quite easy to find potty-training items secondhand, often for free. Parents use these items for a relatively short time and are usually happy to give them away to another family. Check with your local buy/sell/trade groups, or ask around at daycare or preschool to see if anyone has stuff to offload.

Set Up Your Space

As you start acquiring your gear, I recommend getting it set up as soon as you start the rehearsal period. You may have heard that you should hide the new potty until the first day of potty training, because your child will become confused or overly excited if you introduce it too early. In my experience, this theory doesn't hold water.

First of all, lots of kids have older siblings and have lived with floor potties around from the time they were newborns. You don't hear about an epidemic of second children who could never master potty training because of this! In reality, as you practice your Universal Potty Sequence upskills, having the floor potty around can help get your child in the right mindset. They may even ask to sit on the potty, and that's great! Allow them to explore the new items and get them comfortable around the new equipment. However, don't spend too much energy hyping up the new potty—the focus should be on learning about the Universal Potty Sequence and beginning to recognize and label their own body cues, not on these new foreign objects!

In the previous section, we discussed putting some extra props in the bathroom, including wipes, a chair, books, toys, and a spare set of clothes. Parents often ask me if they should be putting a floor potty in the bathroom as well. If you truly have nowhere else to put it, and your child refuses to try out the adult toilet (with whatever seat or insert you've added to make it kid-sized), you can use a floor potty in the bathroom. But I believe this really defeats the purpose of a floor potty, which is to simply have a potty available in rooms that don't have a toilet.

Instead, I want the floor potty set up in whatever room you'll be spending the most time in during day one of potty training. If you have a dedicated playroom in your house, this is where you'll set up the floor potty. If not, think about where your child spends most of their time at home, and set up there. You can also set up a station in their bedroom—this is especially important if your home has multiple levels. You should have one floor potty station set up for each floor that you spend time on. (Nobody has time to scramble up the stairs during the first few days of potty training!)

Wherever you decide to place the potty station, you'll want to prep the area. If you have area rugs, consider rolling them up and putting them in storage for a little while. (Learn from a twin mom I know, who had to throw away two rugs on the first day of potty training!) To protect the floor, you can temporarily lay down washable rugs or throws. If you have carpet, you may want to get some waterproof picnic blankets for easy clean up.

If your couch isn't easily washed, you may also want to drape some throw blankets over the cushions. Some parents will put a waterproof crib mattress protector or puppy pee pads down before covering them with a sheet. One caveat is that I wouldn't make a big deal of these changes for your child, or blame them on potty training. We don't want your kid to think that they're dirty or flawed in any way. You could say you took the rugs to the cleaners, or that you're trying out a new look for the sofa, and casually move on.

Then, make the potty station fun and inviting! Place your child's toys and books nearby so the potty is just part of the room. Make sure there are wipes and cleaning supplies within arm's reach, so you won't have to scramble when there's a mess.

Have Fun with It

Now it's time to bring play-based learning and fun into the process! During the rehearsal period, you should utilize play, books, songs, and even screen time to help your child learn about the potty.

Pretend Play

Get on your kid's level and engage with them during playtime. Find a doll, stuffed animal, or even an action figure and begin a pretend scenario with them. Don't jump right into teaching or your child will smell a rat, but after a few minutes of play, your main character may start to feel a tickle in their tummy . . . does Superman need to go potty?

Here's a more detailed example:

1. Pick a toy to represent a "potty-training friend," who is currently learning to use the potty. If the toy doesn't already have a name, give it a name so it's more relatable for your child. Today, we have "Teddy" the bear as our potty-training friend.

2. Narrate Teddy's actions as it expresses body awareness cues. "Oh, Teddy feels a funny sensation in his tummy. It's time for him to use the potty!" Or wiggle the bear around and say, "Look, Teddy is doing his potty dance. I think he needs to go pee!"

3. Get your child to put Teddy on the floor potty, assist with pulling down his pants (even if they're invisible), and encourage Teddy to mimic relaxing to let out the pee, or blow bubbles to help push out poop.

4. Ask your child questions like "What do you think Teddy feels when he needs to use the potty?" Or "Can you show Teddy how you hold your tummy when you need to go?" (This will help your child recognize and verbalize their own body's sensations in the future.)

Many kids who are resistant to direct instruction will happily engage in play-based learning like this. There's something magical that happens when you externalize the story to a third-party, inanimate object—kids will often express thoughts and worries when talking through a character that they would never blurt out as themselves.

This kind of pretend play can not only help your child learn the steps of pottying, but it can also give you some special insight into how they're feeling leading up to it.

> ### THE POOPING CONCRETE TRUCK
>
> When Auggie was potty training for the second time, I did a lot of pretend play to try and help him connect the dots. He had an extreme interest in big trucks, to the point where he could name all kinds of obscure machines like a hi-rail backhoe and a bucket wheel excavator.
>
> So when it came time to pretend his toys were using the potty, instead of picking an easily anthropomorphized toy like a teddy bear or baby doll, he chose a large concrete mixer truck.
>
> I tried to sway him to use something that actually had a butt, thinking this was a missed opportunity for learning, because how exactly would a truck even sit on the potty?
>
> But he surprised me when he announced, "uh oh, truck feels like a poop is coming!" Then he backed the concrete truck right up to the potty (beeping as it reversed, of course), started rotating its barrel, and, much to my surprise, the truck "pooped" out a whole bunch of Legos.
>
> You better believe I helped the truck finish the Universal Potty Sequence. If you've never wiped the butt of a concrete truck with toilet paper, have you even lived?

Use Props

During playtime, you can teach your child some fundamentals of potty training with unexpected props!

Fill Up a Balloon

Take a small uninflated balloon and tell your kid that you're going to do an experiment at the kitchen sink. Slowly pour water into the balloon. Have your child feel how the balloon gets tighter as the balloon fills up. Explain that the balloon is their bladder, and as they drink water and milk throughout the day, their bladder balloon fills up with water just like this. As the balloon gets REALLY big, talk about how that must be pressing on the inside of their tummy. Then, pinch off the opening and turn the balloon upside down. Ask your kid to help empty the "bladder" by releasing the water. There will likely be lots of giggles, but you've just given them a great visual about how their bladder works!

Raisins in the Pot!

A lot of kids have a fear of the big toilet, and one reason is because the distance from the seat to the water below can seem huge for a small child. This fear can be compounded by the fact that toilet water may splash up on their behinds as they sit. I've consulted with so many families who have this challenge, and they're usually confused by my first follow-up question: do you have any raisins in the house?

I've found that raisins are a great prop to help children experience the big potty in a safe and controlled way. Here's what you do: have your child stand next to the potty with a handful of raisins. Ask them to drop a few into the bowl to watch where they go. Then flush the toilet, and cheer the raisins as they circle the drain! Next, if your child is willing, have them sit on the potty while fully clothed, and ask them to begin dropping raisins into the bowl between the gap in their legs. This simulates what happens when poop falls into the bowl, but in a low-pressure scenario.

Read Books

There are so many adorable and hilarious children's books that are about using the potty! Some favorites include:

- *Potty Time with Elmo* by Sesame Street
- *Daniel's Potty Time* by Daniel Tiger's Neighborhood
- *Let's Go to the Potty* by Alison Jandu

- *A Potty for Me* by Karen Katz
- *Everyone Poops* by Taro Gomi
- *P Is for Potty* by Sesame Street
- *Duck Goes Potty* by Michael Dahl
- *Potty* by Leslie Patricelli
- *Dino Potty* by Rainstorm Publishing
- *We Poop on the Potty!* by Jim Harbison and Nicole Sulgit
- *Potty Time with Bean* by Ms. Rachel

Many children are interested in the science behind going potty. Sure, you're already narrating how they turn food into poop and drinks into pee, but they want to know *how* it happens! Here are a few books that help children understand their anatomy and physiology in an age-appropriate manner:

- *Very First Questions and Answers: What Is Poop?* by Katie Daynes
- *Every Body Poops: Poopy's Great Adventure Through the Body and Beyond* by Colleen A. Simons
- *Look Inside Your Body*, a lift-a-flap board book by Louie Stowell
- New books come out all the time! For an up-to-date list, visit https://goodtogoparenting.com/

Make Your Own Book!

It's easier than you think to create your own personalized children's book (see Table 6.1). Most photo-printing sites have an option to create your own books, or you can download a free template from our website and print it out on a home printer. Your kid is going to be so excited to read a book that features their name and pictures! Combining this kind of personalization with the specifics of the *Good to Go* method will grab a child's attention and help them connect to the process on a deeper level.

Table 6.1 ____*'s Potty Book*

Picture	Text
Picture of your child	_____ is getting ready to learn how to use the potty. Your body makes pee and poop every day. It goes into a diaper, but not for too much longer!
Picture of your child's bathroom	This is _____'s bathroom. This big toilet is where the pee and poop are going to go to be flushed away.
Picture of playroom or bedroom with floor potty	This is where _____ likes to play. See the little potty on the floor? That is there to help catch the pee or poop when you have to go!
Picture of child touching their belly	It all starts with a feeling in your body! Sometimes it feels like a tickle, sometimes it feels like pressure, and sometimes it just feels funny. That is your body telling you it is time to go to the potty. What does it feel like for you?
Picture of child washing their hands	When you feel that tickle, it's time to find a bathroom or your little potty. Pull down your pants and underwear. Now, sit on the toilet and let it out! After, don't forget to wipe until you're all clean. (Mom and dad can help with this part!) Then, it's time to flush it away! Finally, pull up your pants and don't forget to wash your hands!
Picture of a stuffed animal or clothed child sitting on the toilet	Soon you will feel your body giving you a clue to go pee or poop again! It happens a lot during the day! When _____ feels that feeling again, then _____ will sit on the potty. Sometimes pee or poop comes out right away. Sometimes you have to wait a little bit.
Picture of your child in bed	Guess what? You still have your diapers for when you are asleep. When you are sleeping your body still makes pee or poop. That is what your sleep diaper is for. One day you won't need it anymore.
Picture of your child's closet, dresser, or clothing	Learning a new thing takes time! Sometimes the pee or poop misses the potty. If you miss, you can still go to the potty to see if there are any drops left. Then pick out new clothes to wear.
Picture of your child smiling	One of the best parts of learning how to use the potty is feeling proud of yourself! You can say _____ is trying their best and didn't give up!
Family photo	We all work together to help each other learn!

Start by taking pictures of your home and capturing your child posing while practicing various upskills (like flushing or washing their hands), and add them to your book for even more personalization. We've included a sample script here, but you can use your imagination—if your kid loves princesses, throw a few castles and tiaras in the mix; if your kid loves superheroes, make them an action hero in their own story!

Sing Songs

There's a surprising number of catchy songs about going potty that your toddler will be happy to dance along with. (I cannot be held responsible for any earworms that result from listening to these songs!)

- Daniel Tiger—"When You Have to Go Potty, Stop . . . and Go Right Away!"
- Super Simple Songs—"Sitting on the Potty"
- The Kiboomers—"The Potty Song"
- Pinkfong—"Baby Shark's Potty Song"
- CoCo Melon—"Potty Training Song"

Screen Time

Though I don't recommend spending time on screens during the first few days of actual potty training, I do think it can be helpful to watch children's shows that address the topic of going to the bathroom during the rehearsal period. The media landscape changes so fast that it's difficult to recommend specific resources in a book, and I fear any of my recommendations will become outdated right away. Also, I know everyone has different levels of access to various platforms, streaming services, and networks. Instead of listing out specific episodes, I recommend doing a web search for a roundup of the best potty-training episodes and see what pops up, or visit https://goodtogoparenting.com for an updated list.

Should They Go Naked? What about Underwear?

When your child first wakes up, you should remove their sleep diaper right away and take them straight to the bathroom to try to pee, reminding them that this is what you do first thing in the morning, too! First thing in the morning is a great opportunity to "catch" a pee in the potty with little to no effort. Starting the day with this little win can set a good tone for the day and give your child something to be proud of.

Then it's time to get dressed for the day . . . or not? This is the eternal question when it comes to potty-training methods. Should we do a few days totally naked, possibly allowing for a bit more body awareness (and also less laundry)? Or do we put on clothes right away? And what about underwear?

All things being equal, I usually suggest doing at least a day naked from the waist down. The nudity can help connect those crucial body sensations with the visual experience of pottying—even if they miss the potty, they'll get a visual of pee or poop exiting their body. It may be a gross lesson, but it's a useful one!

But things aren't always equal. There are a number of reasons why going naked may not work for your child or your family. One consideration is their temperament: if they are very shy or body conscious, it may be extra stressful for them to be naked. Similarly, if your family has religious or cultural values that frown upon nudity, it may not feel comfortable to have a bare-butted child in your living room 24/7. Another factor is the weather: it may simply be too cold to be naked at the time of potty training, even with the heat cranked up. Potty training is not a good reason to have your child literally freeze their butt off!

If you're not going totally nude, the next question is whether or not to use underwear right away. Again, my default answer is no undies: "going commando" will make the learning process easier for your kid. The logic behind this recommendation is that underwear puts pressure on all the same spots a diaper does. If your child goes straight from diapers to underwear, the tactile sensations they're experiencing around their bottom haven't changed. This could confuse your child into thinking they still have a diaper on and delay their understanding of these new sensation cues.

That said, cute undies can be a strong motivator for many kids. They may know that "big kids wear underwear" and want, so badly, to be a big kid right away. Or they picked out undies with their favorite character on them and cannot wait to wear them. If this is the case, you should harness that enthusiasm. Remember, this is a collaboration, and you want to seize any opportunity for them to be excited about the process. (Also, some kids are so motivated by not wanting to pee on their favorite character that they'll learn faster, just to save Elmo or Spider-Man from getting peed on!)

If your child wants to wear underwear, you're going to set the expectation that if they have a miss and the undies get soiled, they'll need to get washed right away. Using laundry as a scapegoat buys you a few hours to "put away" the underwear and allow your child to practice naked (or commando) in the meantime.

Boxers or Briefs?

Whether or not you start in them, your child will eventually begin to wear underwear! And not all undies are created equal: it's best to choose some that will be conducive to potty training. Some features to look for:

- 100 percent cotton
- Machine washable
- Loose and comfortable waistband and leg holes
- Lay-flat seams (for sensory sensitivities)

Paradoxically, this means you should avoid undies labeled as "potty-training underwear." This style of underwear is designed with extra fabric in the gusset so it's more absorbent. The theory is that this extra-absorbent underwear can act as a bridge between diapers and regular undies, but in my experience it causes more trouble than it's worth. The extra fabric is bulky and makes the underwear tighter around the groin, and may confuse kids into thinking they have a diaper on.

Which style you choose is really up to you. Your child may want to "be like daddy" and wear boxers, or they may want to express their own style. As long as they can manage pulling them up and down on their own, the cut doesn't make much of a difference. That said, boxers and boxer briefs can bunch at the groin, so pay close attention to your child's comfort if they choose that style, and maybe have some briefs on hand as backup.

What about Siblings?

Having siblings can be a double-edged sword when it comes to potty training. On one hand, older siblings or twins can help model and reinforce potty habits, but on the other hand, they can be a huge distraction.

Older Siblings

If your potty-trainee has an older sibling, you can enlist them to help during the rehearsal period! Not only can they provide your younger child with great examples to model from, they can also help with pretend play and preparing your toddler mentally for potty training. Whether it's proudly demonstrating how they recognize their own body cues, reminding their sibling about routine tries, or just cheering them on, a sibling can be an enormous help in this process. You can even give your older child an official "job" during potty training—whether that's being in charge of keeping the toilet paper stocked on the roll, or being the official book reader to your toddler, you'll want to give them simple duties that will make them feel special.

Jealousy may also come into play with an older sibling. Potty training requires a lot of focus from parents, and your older child may notice this temporary shift in attention away from them and toward their younger sibling. This can inspire big feelings and behavior shifts in the other sibling. You can get ahead of this by having a talk with your older child, letting them know that their sibling will be potty training soon, and it may make you extra busy. This is a great time to ask them how they want to be involved—giving them a role in the potty-training journey can turn potential competition into teamwork.

Even if your older kid is on board with the process, they can be unintentionally distracting. Nobody wants to think of their precious child as a distraction, but we all have limits! Even the most independent kids need our attention throughout the day, and having extra children to care for can be overwhelming during the first few days of potty training. If you have the ability, it can be helpful for another adult (whether it's your partner, a grandparent, or babysitter) to plan a fun outing for your older siblings on the first day of potty training. That way, they can have a special activity and you can have the house clear to focus on your toddler.

If that's not possible, try and set your older kids up for as much independent play as you can. Think ahead about how you can minimize your need to leave your toddler's side, and set yourself up for success.

The good news is that having older siblings is a major benefit when it comes to understanding the Universal Potty Sequence. Unlike only children, a younger sibling has spent their entire lives watching another child use the potty. This kind of modeling is more effective to kids because they learn better from their peers (it's more relatable for them to see another child doing something than if they watch an adult). So, even if the older siblings present a logistical challenge during the first few days of potty training, their mere presence has been priming your child for success all along!

I LOVE YOU, NOW GO AWAY

I'm not sure if it's a result of birth order or innate personality, but my older son, Auggie, has always needed more parental attention than his younger brother. When Sebastian was born, a friend told us this adage: "When a second baby is born, first children go from getting

100 percent of their parents' attention to 75 percent, and spend the rest of their lives trying to make up the difference. Meanwhile, the younger sibling is born getting only 25 percent of the attention, and spends the rest of their lives thinking this is sufficient."

This could not be more true in our family. Sebastian has been scarily independent, almost since the day he was born. I have a thirty-minute time-lapse video of him playing independently at six months old. Auggie, on the other hand, loves to rope us into all his pretend play and needs a lot of parental reassurance and intervention. It's fascinating to watch, and I love how different their personalities are.

But when it came time to potty train Sebastian, Auggie's need for parental attention became a bit overwhelming.

Auggie, despite being fully potty trained at this point, still liked to have a parent with him in the bathroom. He didn't need it, per say, but he liked the company. (I've had many a deep conversation about Star Wars while he pooped.) This desire for a bathroom chaperone became a problem on the first day of potty training Sebastian, because I couldn't be in two places at once. And at one point, I had to risk Auggie having a miss because I was trying to teach Sebastian how to release on the floor potty.

Later that day, once Sebastian was peacefully napping in his sleep diaper, I broke down and told my husband that he had a new mission: please, for the love of my sanity, take Auggie somewhere for the afternoon. I love the child, but he needs to leave.

Thankfully, Corey understood the assignment, and he whisked Auggie off to the children's museum for the rest of the day. And though this made Sebastian jealous when he woke from his nap, it did give him a little extra incentive to learn potty independence. I told him, "We're staying home for a little while so you can learn to use the potty. When you start using the potty for a few days, then we can start going on adventures again."

This ended up being a win-win situation: Auggie got some special one-on-one time with his dad (a rarity ever since his brother was born), and I got to be solely focused on helping Sebastian.

Younger Siblings

Many people begin potty training while they also have an infant or young toddler at home. Obviously, with kids this young, you can't exactly give them a job to help with potty training, nor can you easily send them away with a grandparent for the day.

When it comes to timing, I recommend waiting until a new baby is at least three months old before starting potty training another child in the household. If you don't have a deadline (like preschool starting), it's better to wait out the newborn phase. After your whole family has had some time to adjust to the new challenges and routines that come with having a small baby, you will have more bandwidth to tackle the challenge of potty training. The entire family needs this adjustment period: whether you're the birth parent who needs to physically recover, or the older sibling who needs to psychologically accept their new reality, everyone is in a time of transition. There's no need to add another big change to this mix if not absolutely necessary.

Of course, many families don't have this luxury! Whether it's because of a school deadline or because your child's readiness signs are accelerating your timeline, you may need to dive into potty training sooner. Just recognize that it may take a bit longer and be more emotionally and physically draining. Give everyone extra grace and be flexible in the process.

Twins (and Other Multiples)

Just like having older siblings in the house, twins can be both helpful and extra challenging during the potty-training process. Of course, the major difference is that you may be potty training more than one child at the same time!

Any of the upskilling steps can still be done during the rehearsal period, no matter how many kids you're potty training. However, you may want to pick and choose the steps that are easiest to complete when you're pulled in multiple directions. For instance, it may not be prudent to attempt to teach a child how to wipe if you're also in charge of their twin, who wants to learn how to pull down their pants.

But when the actual potty-training day comes, it's time to call in reinforcements. If you have the support, bring in extra adults to help, even assigning one adult per child so you can be totally focused on the process. If additional help isn't available, you may want to consolidate your life into one room. One twin mom I talked to said she put up baby gates around her living room and spent the first forty-eight hours of potty training there (minus naps and bedtime, of course). She also made sure to have at least four floor potties available—one in each corner—so her twins had easy and quick access when they needed to go.

With twins, even though it's going to be twice as messy, I recommend doing potty training at the same time. The twins can reinforce each other's skills and provide a textbook model of peer-to-peer learning!

If you have higher-order multiples, you may consider potty training them separately. You may focus on a child that is showing more signs of readiness than the others first and then potty-train them in succession.

Tandem Training

If you have two children who are less than two years apart, there's a chance you may end up potty training them simultaneously. It may just happen without your influence! I've seen this happen more times than you'd expect—a family comes to me for help with training their previously reluctant 3.5-year-old, only to discover their 2-year-old ends up learning right alongside their sibling!

This is definitely possible, but not always the best course of action. Just like with twins, potty training two siblings with an age gap can make the process extra complicated. You'll be balancing two different personalities and two different skill levels. If the process happens naturally, with the younger sibling learning by observing and having an intrinsic desire to also start using the potty, more power to them. But I wouldn't force this scenario except for in very rare circumstances.

However, if both of your children are ready, and especially if you have the same deadline (say, you're going back to full-time work and are putting them in the same diaper-free preschool), this could be an option to consider. Just read through the section above about twins and multiples for specific tips.

THE YOUNGER SISTER INFLUENCE

My brother, Jeff, is twenty months older than me. But it's family lore that, even though I was almost two years younger than him, I potty trained first. (This is a story my brother hated as a teenager, which is understandable.)

The story goes that my mom had been trying to potty train Jeff for over a year, with very little luck. He was successfully peeing in the potty most of the time, but he absolutely refused to poop on the toilet. My brother was only three and a half, and wasn't in preschool (my grandma, a total saint and one of the best women to ever walk this earth, provided my mom with free childcare), so there was no pressure for him to start. My mom was incredibly busy, a physician working more than full time as a pediatric geneticist, and didn't have the bandwidth to really push potty training, anyway.

Meanwhile, I was approaching two years old and a bit precocious. Unlike Jeff, who was perfectly happy staying in diapers, I apparently decided I wanted to use the potty. I started pulling my diapers off and, according to my mom, I "potty trained myself" before I turned two.

Somehow, I doubt it was some miraculous, overnight decision I made for myself. I suspect my grandma probably did some direct teaching. Or maybe I just was present for every lesson given to my brother and thought they were meant for me, too.

Whatever the motive, I started using the potty for both pee and poop before him. And, in a classic older brother move, he decided this injustice would not stand. My mom said that as soon as he saw me using the potty, Jeff started using the potty, too. All he needed was some sibling competition to get over the potty-training hump.

Prepare for Big Emotions

Learning something new is incredibly difficult. Learning to use the potty requires both physical and mental effort, which can be very draining for your child!

While your child is busily using their body and their brain to master this new skill, their emotions may end up totally out of whack. They may become downright dysregulated, showing signs of stress or "acting out" in ways you're not used to. Tantrums may become more frequent, or they may have a short fuse. On the flip side, your child may become extra sensitive or comfort-seeking.

Every child will react differently, but it's best to be prepared for these mood changes. Remind yourself that your child is working hard, and that they deserve grace. Try to remember how you felt when studying for your first big exam in a new school. Synthesizing new knowledge while also being in a new environment can be very stressful.

One way to prepare for these mood swings is to create an emotional hygiene routine for your child, as discussed in Chapter 2, "The Big Picture." And just being ready to provide extra love and emotional support during this time will help everyone stay regulated and calm. During potty training, you may want to pick your battles with your toddler and stop sweating the small stuff. The more you can reduce stress, the better.

To Stand or to Sit, That Is the Question

If your child has a penis, you may be wondering whether they should pee standing up. After all, most adult men in their lives likely stand to pee, and this is the norm in most countries.

There's actually a fair amount of cultural variation in whether a man stands or sits. A 2023 YouGov survey asked over 7,000 men from thirteen countries how often they sit to urinate. This poll found that

40 percent of men in Germany sit every time, while that number is only 10 percent in the United States.

Just like there's differences between countries, every family's culture is going to be different when it comes to this decision. There's no "right" answer here, just some pros and cons for each side. Let's explore those:

Sitting Advantages

- *Less mess:* sitting can reduce splashes, spills, or aim issues, making clean-up easier for parents. This is especially true with a floor potty, as the bowls tend to be shallow and narrow compared to large toilets.
- *Combo bonus:* poop and pee can come out at the same time, which is often the case for new learners.
- *More focus:* kids can read a book and be more relaxed while sitting on the potty.
- *More time:* if your child is taking some time to figure out releasing their pee, sitting gives them more time to figure it out.
- *More stable:* standing to pee requires balance, control, and an ability to stay still for long enough to aim the urine into the bowl. Sitting doesn't require as much motor control.

Sitting Disadvantages

- *Future transitions:* eventually, boys will likely want to learn to pee while standing up, so they may need to be taught this skill over again.
- *Confusion:* if they're always sitting, they may become confused when they are encouraged to stand in other situations (like public restrooms with a urinal).
- *Peer approval:* other boys (at preschool) may tease your child about sitting to pee, causing social discomfort and pressure to change.

Standing Advantages

- *Future readiness:* they will already know how to use urinals, which are common in public places.
- *Speed:* once boys master standing, peeing is a quick process and can be done in a hurry.
- *Builds coordination:* standing to pee helps develop balance and aim.

Standing Disadvantages

- *More mess:* urine tends to splash all over, especially when they are first learning. Also, the final drips of urine may fall on their feet, causing discomfort.
- *Less relaxed:* standing can feel rushed and uncomfortable, resulting in a kid who can't relax enough to release their urine.
- *Steeper learning curve:* standing, aiming, and controlling their urine flow requires more focus and is harder to learn, especially for young toddlers. This may be discouraging and hinder the learning process.

If all things are equal, and you don't have a strong preference either way, I would recommend starting by sitting on the potty. Unless your child asks to pee standing up, sitting has been an easier point of entry for most of my students.

Whatever you decide, remember that when your child sits on the potty to poop, they will likely have some urine come out at the same time. Teach your child to push their penis downward every time they sit, even if they don't think they need to pee. This small habit really pays off when it comes to cleaning up!

Stream Direction and Phimosis

If your child's penis is not circumcised, there is no need to pull back the foreskin before urinating. You should never forcibly retract your child's foreskin, and most children won't be able to retract before the age of five.

Often, potty training is the first time we can really observe our children in the act of peeing. (Another opportunity tends to be when they first get into a bath, though they're often underwater when this happens.) When an uncircumcised child is peeing, you may notice the urine stream coming out at an angle, and this angle may change every time they pee! This is totally normal, and just a result of the way the foreskin is positioned at the tip of the penis. You may also notice some bulging or ballooning on the end or side of his penis while he pees, which is also completely normal. Young children tend to have tight foreskin, which explains both of these things.

A tight foreskin isn't considered a problem unless there are other symptoms like:

- Swelling, tenderness, or redness
- Blood in the urine
- Frequent urinary tract infections
- Bleeding or thick discharge from under the foreskin, or an unpleasant smell
- Pain while peeing
- Blocked urine or weak flow

This last item, having a weak flow, can also present as not having a steady stream of urine. If your child's pee comes out in multiple streams, similar to when you place your thumb over a water hose, this could be a sign of a condition known as phimosis. In fact, all the above are symptoms of phimosis, and you should bring this up with your child's physician if you have any concerns.

How to Pass the Time

The first few days of potty training can be both exciting and tedious. Ideally, you'll be staying close to home and avoiding screen time, which means you'll be spending a lot of time doing . . . what, exactly?

Having some activities ready to go can be super helpful to avoid boredom. Most of these suggestions have minimal setup and don't require buying anything new—you can play these with items you already own.

- *Toy Hide and Seek*: You don't want to play traditional hide and seek while potty training (unless you want a pee puddle in your closet), but you can play this classic game with your child's toys or other household objects. It's best to limit this to a single room so they don't end up too far from their floor potty. Ask them to close their eyes and count as high as they can (great numbers practice while you're at it!), hide a toy, then let them loose to find it. Give them "warmer" and "colder" proximity cues, and celebrate when they find it. Or your child can do the hiding!

- *Obstacle Course*: Create a simple obstacle course with pillows, chairs, and blankets. Have your child crawl under tables, jump over pillows, or balance on a line of painter's tape you've put on the floor. Getting them moving can be really helpful to let out energy and also to help stimulate bowel movements!

- *Animal Charades*: Take turns pretending to be different animals. Act out how they move and the sounds they make. Ask your child to guess which animal you're being, and then guess what they're acting out!

- *Sock Toss*: Play basketball with balled-up socks and a laundry basket. You can assign points based on distance, or mark spots on the floor with painter's tape to indicate different levels of difficulty.

- *Simon Says*: This one's a classic! Give your child simple commands, starting with the key phrase: "Simon says jump on one foot." "Simon says touch the tip of your nose." Then, of course, you slip in a non-Simon-says command to try and trick them: "Shake your head." Kids absolutely love this game, but what they love even more is being the person giving the commands! Take turns and come up with some wacky instructions.

- *Eye Spy*: Spot an item in the room and pick a single adjective to describe it. "I spy with my little eye something green." Have your child guess what you spied, then take turns.

- *Dance Party*: Turn on some music and just dance! You can take turns picking songs or even play the "freeze dance" by pausing the music occasionally. All the bouncing around from dancing can really help your child feel the pee sensation!

- *Storytime Theater*: Act out one of your child's favorite stories using props found around the house. A blanket can be a princess cape, or a wooden spoon can become a pirate sword. Let them choose one of the characters and join in.

- *Indoor Bowling*: Set up empty water bottles or paper towel tubes to use as bowling pins, and use a soft ball to knock them down.

- *What's on My Back?*: This one is for all the tired parents out there. Lie face down on the couch or floor and ask your child to place a small object on your back. Then, without touching it, try to figure out what they put on your back. You can take turns, but your child will probably love continuing to surprise you, and you get the bonus of lying down!

Chapter in Review

- Separate sleep and waking diapers to limit confusion around daytime and nighttime training.
- Select clothes that are easy to get in and out of.
- Stock up with the right gear, including floor and travel potties.
- Arrange your home to make potty training as easy and accessible as possible, with floor potties in play areas and rugs rolled up and stored away.

- Utilize the power of play, reading, and even making your own books.
- Underwear on day one is a game-time decision—if it motivates your child, use it!
- Consider the role and influence of siblings and get them on board or out of the way.
- Learning anything new can take its toll. Keep an eye out for mood swings, more or less hunger, and sleep disruptions.

7

It's Go Time

You've spent weeks practicing your upskills, modeling and narrating the heck out of your potty habits, and prepping your house and child for this moment. Now, it's go time! Let's go over the step-by-step plan for removing daytime diapers and exactly how to manage any challenges that come your way.

Body Awareness Is the #1 Goal

On the first day, the name of the game is simply connecting your child's internal cues to the need to physically sit on the potty. This is step 1 of the Universal Potty Sequence (UPS), as discussed in previous chapters, and it's all we're focused on today.

We all have three different types of awareness that help us cue into our potty needs. *Sensation awareness* was already discussed in detail in Chapter 3, "Rethinking Readiness." If you recall, this type of awareness refers to knowing whether a potty event has happened, is happening, or is about to happen.

Action awareness is knowing the difference between the need to urinate or have a bowel movement. Simply: do I need to pee or do I need to poop? Most kids don't need much help differentiating between these two sensations, but it's important to keep this in mind for later on, when you start prompting or interpreting their external cues.

Urgency awareness is your child's ability to predict how much time they have before they need to go. When we start potty training, your kid is not going to have much, if any, urgency awareness. It always starts at an emergency level—if they realize they need to go, it has to happen right away! This is why it's so important to have floor potties available nearby. With time and repetition, they'll develop the skill to predict further out. But, for now, the sooner you can physically get them to a potty, the better.

In the first few days, learning is going to be messy. Though you may think of failed potty attempts as "accidents," I find it more constructive and accurate to call them "misses." An accident is something that happens to you, outside of your control. But when you "miss," you still are given credit for trying. Even if pee gets on the floor, you can help your kid complete the other steps of the UPS and try again another time.

Three Types of Body Awareness

Sensation Awareness
"I feel a tickle"

Action Awareness
Is this a pee or a poop?

Urgency Awareness
How much time do I have?

LAURA MISSES THE MARK

Look, when Gia told me to stop using the word "accidents" and replace it with "misses," I, too, was super skeptical. I had used "accidents" with my older son, Auggie, and never thought about it as shaming or demoralizing. Everyone around me understood "accidents" and used it casually, as well. But, when it came time to potty train Sebastian, I trusted Gia's expertise and vowed to switch to "misses" and remove "accidents" from my vocabulary.

It wasn't easy. When you discover your child standing in pee-soaked pants, it's tough to have the cognitive flexibility to not only address the mess and regulate your own emotions, but also change up language patterns you've used for years. More than once, I found myself saying, "Oh, honey, looks like you had an acci–MISS. A MISS. Yep, that's a MISS!" All this just to try and rewire my own brain to use this new terminology. I must admit, I wondered whether it was worth the effort.

Then, one day, I heard my son's adorable little voice call to me from the next room, "mama, I have miss!" This was a few weeks into potty training, and at that point, he wasn't having misses very often. I found him standing in a puddle of pee, a little sheepish but not ashamed. I took him to the bathroom to try and finish the potty sequence, and, lo and behold, he still had to poop! He was so happy that he got to convert a "miss" into a win. "I miss, but now I poop in the potty!" He proudly exclaimed. There was something incredibly charming and disarming about his innocent way of announcing the issue. Hearing the term "miss" from him really helped me realize how non judgmental the term was, and how he wasn't ashamed or embarrassed about it.

From that point on, I was fully on board with "misses"—even if they still sometimes come out as "acci-MISSES."

The Highly Involved Phase

In Chapter 2, "The Big Picture," we introduced the concept of parental involvement being on a spectrum, starting with a highly involved phase and eventually ending in being rarely or never involved. Guess what? You've made it to the highly involved phase!

So what does this mean, exactly? It means your child is relying on you for significant support in their learning process. In a way, you're going to be acting as an external, second brain for them. I'm borrowing this idea from how we discuss emotional co-regulation as "borrowing" someone's calm nervous system. I like to imagine parents lending their brains and experience to their children during this highly involved phase.

What this means, in practice, is that you are going to be on high alert for signs that your child needs to go potty. Here are some common signs you may observe:

- Frequent fidgeting or changing positions
- Doing a "potty dance" or crossing legs
- Touching, grabbing, or holding their genitals
- A penis that is semi-erect or larger than usual

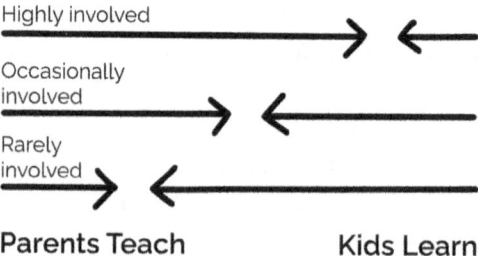

- Grimacing, concentrating, or sudden changes in facial expressions
- Becoming very still after being active
- Going to a corner or another room for privacy
- Saying words like "potty," "uh-oh," or "oops"
- Becoming more clingy or seeking a parent's attention
- Squatting down and grunting
- Farting/Passing gas
- Suddenly being extra grumpy or mad—a.k.a. acting "pissy"

LAURA DISCOVERS THE TRUE ORIGIN OF "PISSY"

Now that Auggie has been potty trained for a few years, I've noticed a pattern: when he really needs to go, he becomes kind of a jerk.

Don't get me wrong, I love my son to the moon and back, and I think he's an awesome person. All kids get moody at times, that's to be expected. But there's been a correlation between times he's been holding in pee or poop—usually because he's too engrossed in his Legos to stop playing—and him being snippy, short-tempered, and just plain grumpy.

Before I made this connection, I always attributed it to him being tired or hungry. But time and time again, I discovered he'd use the bathroom and his mood would become sunny again. Was he literally "in a pissy mood" because he needed to go potty?

Of course, I had to research this. I already knew (thanks to the last season of *Succession* on HBO) that urinary tract infections can cause some serious cognitive symptoms that can even mimic dementia. Could this bladder-brain connection be responsible for mood changes on a smaller scale?

It turns out, there's a burgeoning field of study trying to figure this out! In 2023, researchers published a paper in the *International*

> *Journal of Molecular Sciences* investigating the correlation between lower urinary tract symptoms and depression. And there's an established connection between anxiety and having an "overactive bladder." It seems the relationship can go both ways.
>
> So, the next time your kid is acting grumpy or irritable and you can't figure out the cause, maybe ask them if they need to potty!

When you see a sign, encourage them to sit on the potty right away. You may even want to bring the floor potty right to them so they can sit on it quickly.

You may not get much warning when it comes to pee, and that's okay! The lead time between a child noticing the urge to pee and actually releasing is going to be extremely short at the beginning. As your child develops, this lead time stretches out, giving you more of a chance to "catch" the pee in the potty.

Poop, however, is a bit of a different story. While pee comes out quickly, poop takes a little more effort, and this can be used to your advantage. You get more time to notice your child's cues and have more lead time to get them to a potty.

Expect some pushback from your kid—it's natural. You're going to need to balance encouragement with their need for autonomy. If

Urgency Awareness Lead Time

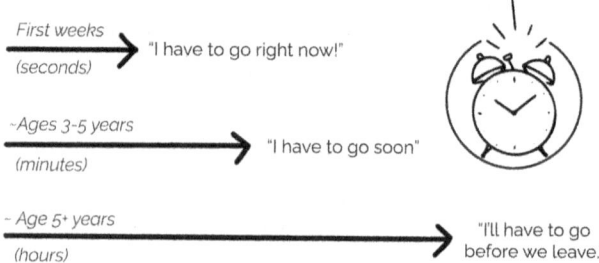

they're adamantly resisting going to the potty, even though you're *certain* they have to go, you may need to let this one be a miss and reevaluate your approach. We need to be mindful of the link between stress and withholding; keeping the atmosphere stress-free is more important than some misses, especially at the beginning.

If you suspect your child needs to go, but they're in denial or unaware, you can engage them with talk about bodily sensations, anxieties, or external cues you may see:

- "When you press your belly, do you feel any pee?"
- "When you feel the poop feeling, you don't have to hide. You can have privacy in the bathroom."
- "Did you know your bladder fills up like a cup? You pour it out when you pee in the potty. Is your bladder feeling a bit full, or like SUPER full, almost to the brim? It feels different!"
- "Did you hear that fart? Sometimes farts means a poop is coming soon!"
- "Jump up and down and see if you have any pee tickles?"

You may have heard that you shouldn't "remind" your child to use the potty and instead just sit back and let them try and figure out the process by trial and error. Some experts claim if you prompt your child before they feel the urge to go, that you're robbing your child of the chance to connect their body's cues to the need to potty. But a child needs to develop their sensation and urgency awareness skills before they can learn to initiate a trip to the potty. By helping them connect the dots, you're not depriving them of the chance to develop this skill, you're just providing them with direct instruction and a good foundation for learning.

Expect Resistance

When reading through the prompts in the previous section, was your first reaction "oh, my kid will never just answer me straight!" A lot of children are going to resist questions and prodding, especially when it comes to bodily functions. And, for what it's worth, there's no way to *force* your child to go potty.

There are three key areas where a child's body sovereignty overrules parental pressure: eating, sleeping, and going to the bathroom. Unless you're force-feeding a child, they are the ultimate decision-makers of whether or not something goes in their mouth. Same thing goes for sleeping: no matter how much you desperately need them to sleep, there's nothing you can do to make them sleep. You can support them with great sleep hygiene, a flawless bedtime routine, sing them soothing songs, and read the most boring stories, but you can't hold their eyelids closed and *make* them fall asleep.

Pottying is the same story. You can sit your child on the potty, you can give them all the support and encouragement in the world, but you can't make their pelvic floor muscles relax to release pee or poop. There's only so much you can do.

What we can do is tap into the three-step negotiation skills we learned in Chapter 2, "The Big Picture." Here's how that may play out during potty training.

You start noticing some signs that your kid needs to pee. They're currently engrossed with building a tower of magnetic tiles, but they've started wiggling and doing a clear "potty dance." You suggest, "I see you're wiggling around, let's check and see if there's a pee-pee ready to come out!" But your child resists, "No! I want to play!" Now is where we begin the three steps.

The Negotiation Sequence

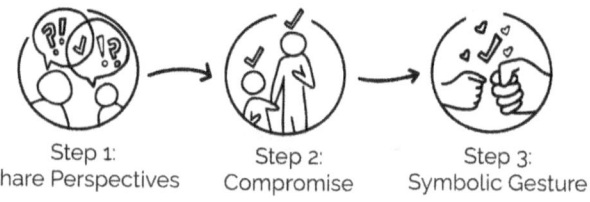

Step 1: Share Perspectives   Step 2: Compromise   Step 3: Symbolic Gesture

Step 1: Share Perspectives

Remember, this is the *connection* part of the process. "Wow, honey, of course you don't want to stop playing. Look at this amazing tower you built! I see all kinds of colors and it's sooooo tall! You know, I wouldn't want to stop building this either." Now, add in your own perspective. "I want you to try to potty. I know you don't like it when you have a miss." Most likely, your child will push back, and be self-focused ("but I don't need to potty!"), but this is where you encourage them to repeat your perspective back. "I heard you, but did you hear me? I want you to try to go potty." The goal is for your child to be able to say, "Daddy wants me to try."

Step 2: Teach Compromise

Now that you understand each other's perspective, a compromise needs to be agreed upon. Encourage your kid to feel heard in this process:

> Parent: "I want us to take a break and go potty, but you want to keep playing. What should we do?"
> Child: "Keep playing!"
> Parent: "Okay, but I'm worried you'll have a miss, and that may mess up the tower you built. Here's an idea: would you like to bring some magnetic tiles to the bathroom with you? We can put them on the counter while you try to pee. Or, we could use the floor potty in here, what do you think?"
> Child: "Use the floor potty!"
> Parent: "Okay, that seems like a deal!"

Step 3: Seal the Deal

Remember, we like to seal the deal with a handshake (or some other symbolic gesture) to help solidify the agreement between parent and child. Once you do that, there's no going back on the agreement. In a situation like this, if you suspect your child may still push back and refuse to sit on the potty, you may want to clearly spell out a consequence if they go back on the deal. "Okay, deal, I'll go get the floor potty and you'll try to pee. If you don't, we may have to take a break from playing so we don't miss and get pee on the magnetic tiles."

Pause the Screen Time

This early phase of potty training requires a lot of focus from both you and your child. You're both keeping an eye out for cues and trying to catch as many pees and poops as possible in the potty. Sometimes, you may only have a few seconds of warning before your child needs to go. With such a short lead time, anything that pulls your attention in a different direction can affect the learning process.

Obviously, there are distractions in our daily life that we can't control. Meals need to be prepared, dogs need to be walked, and parents need to go to the bathroom themselves, even! But one thing we *can* control is our screen time use.

During this highly involved phase, I encourage parents to put their phones away as much as possible. Similarly, avoid screen time for your child, if at all possible. Adults and children alike can get completely sucked into the screen and miss important opportunities for learning. Once your child starts connecting the dots and begins giving you a little more advanced warning that they need to go, you can reintroduce screen time as appropriate (for both of you!)

LAURA DITCHES HER PHONE

During the first day of potty training Sebastian, I was feeling pretty confident. After all, I had been working with Gia to develop her *Good to Go* method and felt like an emerging expert on the topic. I had made all my newbie-parent mistakes with his older brother, Auggie, and was ready to absolutely crush potty training this second time around.

I was definitely humbled when the first morning did not go as planned. I had done all the prep work and was following Gia's method to a T, but somehow Sebastian kept missing! By noon, I had already cleaned up two pee puddles off our playroom floor and my confidence was starting to flag.

As Sebastian played with his Duplos in the corner, I felt my phone vibrate with a few new work emails in my inbox. I had officially taken the day off to focus on potty training, but Sebastian was content and quiet, so I thought I could quickly respond to these messages. And, honestly, I was bored. My phone seemed like an alluring distraction from a stressful morning.

Okay, so it's possible I drifted over to social media after I finished those emails. I'm only human. But as I scrolled, I heard Sebastian say, "uh oh, mama." I looked up from my phone to see Sebastian standing above pee puddle #3 of the day.

I cringed. Not because of the floor pee (thank goodness for hardwood), but because I had clearly missed an opportunity to help him. Sebastian wasn't the one having the misses here, it was me.

After that incident, I decided I couldn't be trusted around my phone. I told Sebastian that mommy had been distracted, but I was going to pay more attention going forward. I then put my phone on do-not-disturb mode and placed it on the highest shelf of our tallest bookcase. Out of sight, out of mind. And I'm happy to report that this simple tactic worked. For the rest of the day, I was able to focus more on Sebastian and really lean into the concept of being in the "highly involved phase." A few hours later, I noticed him shifting his weight from leg to leg, and noticed it as a cue. I took him over to the floor potty in the corner of the playroom, and we caught our first pee of the day, with no screens in sight.

The Night Before

On the eve of potty training, you're going to let your child know exactly what's going to happen. Remember, you're working as a team in this situation! As you put them in their sleeping diaper, you can tell them that when they wake up in the morning, they won't be putting on daytime diapers like usual. Keep it encouraging and supportive: "We've been talking about you going pee/poop in the potty, and tomorrow, we will start together. It might be tricky at first, but I will be here to help you."

If you sense your child is feeling sentimental about this, you can make a ritual of gathering up the daytime diapers and putting them away together. (I don't recommend throwing them away, as this places a lot of pressure on kids, and may spike their anxiety.) Then, show them that the nighttime diapers are still available for naps and nighttime.

You'll want to have multiple changes of easy-to-remove clothing ready and waiting. Think: a couple of pairs of loose, elastic-waisted pants or a few short dresses. Also, consider wearing water-resistant, washable shoes, like Crocs, Natives, or swim shoes (fabric shoes will take a long time to dry and nobody wants to wear soggy pee shoes!). Whether or not your kid ends up naked tomorrow, you want to be prepared so you don't have to rush to do laundry.

Day One: Sample Schedule

What an exciting and nerve-wracking day! You're now equipped with the knowledge and skills to tackle potty training, but you may be confused at how you actually go about it, minute by minute, hour by hour.

This process can be overwhelming, even for the most prepared parent. Because of this, I wanted to provide you with a sample schedule for what your first day of potty training may look like. This is meant to be descriptive, not prescriptive. I don't live with you, I don't know what time your kid actually wakes up! But hopefully this general breakdown will help you feel more confident about how you approach your day!

7:00 a.m.—Rise and Shine!

- Start the day with some cuddles and a cheerful morning reminder that today is the day!
- Ask them to pat their diaper. Does it feel full?
- Walk over to the bathroom together to take it off and see what's inside. Is it gushy with pee? Is there a poop inside?
- Invite them to sit on the potty and see if there are any surprise pee pee sprinkles left in their bladder. This is the first routine try of the day.
- If they're going naked, remind them why: to help them notice their body's cues!
- If they are excited to put on their new underwear, by all means, put them on! But this is a great time to remind them of the plan: if the undies get soiled, they'll go into the wash and your child will be naked until they're clean again.

7:30 a.m.—Breakfast

- Is your child still in a high chair? Or a seat? Either way a bare butt will not be comfortable. Line the seat with a puppy pad or towel.
- As you eat breakfast, talk about how you will be spending your day: "Today we will play at home while you are learning to listen to your body. We might go for a little walk to see how that feels. What are you looking forward to about today?"

8:00 a.m.—Playtime

- Hang out in the designated areas of your house that you have prepared (see Chapter 6, "Set the Stage").

- Keep a floor potty near you at all times.
- Watch for signs that they may have to use the potty.
- Ask your child:
  - "Is your bladder giving you any clues?"
  - "Do you feel like you need to fart? Sometimes that means poop is coming soon."
- It is highly likely that sometime before wake-up and snack they will need to go! Either wait for a body cue or just give a prompt if you think enough time has passed.
- Ask body-sensation questions like:
  - "Jump up and down and see if you have any pee tickle?"
  - "Wiggle your bottom, do you feel anything sloshing around?"
- If they are not connecting the dots yet, shift to asking a prompt like "We are going to try to go potty. It's okay if you don't pee or poop. We will keep practicing together. Let's get your book and read it on the potty."

10:00 a.m.—Snack

- Same thing as breakfast: line the seat, not the child.
- Do a little re-teach about how the body works:
  - "When we drink a lot of water to stay hydrated, that means we will make a lot of pee pee!"
  - "Once this snack goes into our stomach and through our bellies, our bodies will take what it needs to give you energy, and the rest will come out as poop!"

10:30 a.m.—Emotional Hygiene Practice

- Spend five minutes in your cozy corner practicing one emotional-regulation technique (see Chapter 2, "The Big Picture").

10:35 a.m.—More Playtime

- Try one of the easy, no-prep games we listed in Chapter 6, "Set the Stage."

- Let's say, by this time of the day your child has had their first miss. Remember the gift of the *Good to Go* method is that a miss is only one step of potty training. Simply grab the nearest floor potty and catch what you can and then complete the sequence: sit, try, wipe, flush, change clothes (if applicable), wash hands. You could say:

    – "You missed, let's finish using the potty."
    – Invite them to help you mop up whatever dribbles there are but no need to force it. It's important that they understand they're not "in trouble" or receiving any kind of punishment for a miss. After all, they still could complete steps 2–9 of the UPS!

- Use descriptive praise for when they go in the potty:

    – "You listened to your body."
    – "You pushed your pants down all by yourself."

- Acknowledge misses by saying something like:

    – "We get some, we miss some. You are still learning."
    – "Let's do the rest."
    – "Want a hug? Learning new things takes time."

12:00 p.m.—Lunch

- There's no need to push extra fluids or encourage salty foods. Just make lunch and offer their water, milk, or juice as you would normally.

- As you are eating, you can get your child mentally prepared for the upcoming routine try, which will happen right before naptime.

- Also explain that they will have a naptime diaper for when they are sleeping. You can say, "You can't hear your body when you are sleeping, so you will have a sleep diaper."

12:30 p.m.—Post-Lunch Potty Break

- Time for another routine try. You can say, "We always try to use the potty before going to sleep even if we don't have the feeling. Let's see what happens when you try."
- Consider reading a book to them for a few minutes while they are sitting on the potty, to help pass the time.
- Whether or not they pottied, finish the UPS and then put on their sleep diaper.

1:00 p.m.—Naptime

- Get your child settled for a nap in their sleep diaper.
- Now is a great opportunity to fill your child's emotional cup:
  - Tell them you're proud of them for working so hard at learning a new skill.
  - Remind them that sleep is when their brains store memories and when they wake up they'll be even smarter.

2:30 p.m.—Wake Up and Potty Check

- As soon as they wake, ask them to squeeze their diaper. "Did pee pee come out while you were asleep?" If yes, go to the bathroom to complete the rest of the UPS.
- If not, say, "Wow, I bet there is some pee pee ready to come out now! Let's go!"

3:00 p.m.—Snack Time

- Same as before, but this time say something like "We have played at home and you have been trying to listen to your body this whole time. I wonder what going on a walk would be like? Want to try?"

4:00 p.m.—Afternoon Walk (optional)

- Potty training can make you stir crazy, so I suggest a short walk in the afternoon to break up the monotony. Don't go far (five minutes each way at most), and don't use a stroller. This is just to get your blood moving.

- Even though it's been a short time since the last routine try, this is a good time to emphasize the need for a routine try any time you plan to leave the house.

- If naked, put pants or shorts on with no underwear underneath. Since you're not going far, don't bring backup clothes, but be aware that you may have to carry a wet child for a few minutes if there's a miss while you're out.

- If you're comfortable with it, you could bring the travel potty along, or a disposable urinal bag.

- On your walk, just take a break from worrying about potty training and enjoy the fresh air.

- When you get back home, if your child didn't pee before you left (even though they tried) and didn't pee on the walk, then say, "We just got home. Let's give it a try!"

- You may decide to skip the walk and stay home. If you have outdoor space, then drag the floor potty outside and play outdoors for a while. Otherwise, follow the same steps as you did during morning playtime.

- Besides routine tries, only use timed invitations or prompts at most once an hour.

- There may be another miss during this time, but you know what to do!

5:30 p.m.—Dinner Prep

- While you make dinner, you will shift your highly involved focus off of your child and onto another task. Prep your child by saying:
  - "I'm going to be in the kitchen making dinner, but you can still listen to your body while I'm in the other room! You can always call for help if you have the pee feeling and I will come right away! And the floor potty is right here next to you if you need it!"
- Or, if it's in budget and you're not feeling like cooking, order delivery! It's okay to take steps to reduce your own stress during this process. If ordering out isn't possible (too expensive or no delivery service available), plan ahead by doing meal prep or doubling your night-before meal for easy leftovers.

6:00 p.m.—Dinner Time

- Follow the same steps from breakfast and lunch.
- While having dinner, engage in conversation about "What did I learn today?" but make sure every member of the family takes a turn. For example, one parent can say, "I learned that my friend is moving to another city, and I am going to miss them." A sibling might say, "I learned the colors of the rainbow." And you can encourage your potty-training toddler to say, "I am learning how to use the potty."

6:30 p.m.—Bath Time

- After dinner, I suggest going straight into bath time because there is a routine try built in.
- While the watering is running, have your child sit on the potty for a routine try and see if anything is ready to come out! The sound of rushing water can often stimulate a pee.

- Time to get into the bath! Sometimes, if they did not pee before, the warm water will release their pee. If that happens, have them focus on the sensation and say something like "What did it feel like right before the pee came out? That will be your body's clue for next time."
- After the bath go ahead and put on their sleep diaper right away. You've both done enough hard work for the day!

7:00 p.m.—Wind-Down and Bedtime Routine

- During your regular wind-down routine, they may go in their sleep diaper or they may ask to use the potty on their own.
- Stick to your usual routine: brushing teeth, books, songs, and so on. Your child has been working hard to learn new things, and sticking to an otherwise predictable routine will be reassuring.
- If they didn't pee before the bath, right before bed, say, "We always try to pee before going to sleep!" This is another opportunity for a routine try. Many kids have a poop right before bed, after their dinner has had some time to digest. Reading a bedtime book while they sit may be helpful.

8:00 p.m.—Going to Sleep

- Now they are diapered and all tucked in! You may notice that they're extra tired: that's a normal side effect of learning something new!
- Review the day together. Share what progress you saw, listen to what thoughts your child has, and think about tomorrow.
  - "Today you didn't have diapers and you were learning to use the potty. What was that like?"
  - "I saw you stop when you noticed pee was coming out."
  - "You are working very hard to learn a new thing!"

- Maybe share a story about something new you have learned recently!
- "How was your first day without diapers?"

What If I Need to Leave the House?

In our sample schedule, we only left the house for a few minutes to take a walk down the block. But what if you really need to go somewhere?

There are plenty of valid reasons for needing to leave the house on day one. Maybe you need to pick up an older sibling from school, and you don't have anyone else to watch your potty-training kid at home. Or maybe you discovered you're out of milk, and your toddler won't go to bed without a glass.

If you find yourself in a situation where you must leave the house with your kid, it's okay to put them in a pull-up for the duration of the short outing. While I think it can be a little confusing for children to put a diaper back on, you can mitigate this by talking through the situation with your child. "We have to drive to pick up your brother. You've been doing an amazing job working on going pee and poop in the potty, but we're going to take a break just while we drive to pick up. I don't want you to worry about going potty in the car seat."

Make sure you have your travel potty available, and give yourself extra time just in case your toddler announces that they want to use the potty and you have to pull over.

When you get home, remove the diaper and tell them they're back to learning. If they used their diaper during the outing, complete the steps of the Universal Potty Sequence like you did during the rehearsal period.

If you planned to potty train on a specific weekend and then get invited to a birthday party or other event, I would urge you to really consider if it's necessary to attend. While I've had a client who successfully managed to bring their toddler to a three-hour kid's birthday party on day one of potty training, this is the exception, not the rule. Parties and large events can be overwhelming and take children out of their regular routines. This type of excitement can be disruptive to the learning process and can make potty training take longer.

In the next chapter, I will talk more about how to introduce longer outings. In the near future, you'll be able to resume your normal life again, I promise! The sacrifices you're making right now are worthwhile and temporary.

The End of Day One

Once your child is in bed, happily snoozing in their sleep diaper, it's time for you to celebrate! No matter how well you think today went, you did some hard work and you deserve a pat on the back.

You may want to reflect on how you feel right now. It's possible your body is holding on to stress, anxiety, or extra energy. Pour yourself a beverage that helps you relax, and try to find ways to get yourself back into a regulated space. For some people, that could mean watching a reality show or soaking in the bathtub. For others, it could mean doing some organizing or house cleaning to feel in control.

Whatever you do, I want you to feel proud for all the intentionality of your efforts today. You just gave your child an amazing gift by beginning potty training in a respectful and collaborative way. Congratulations on being awesome!

Chapter in Review

- Day one is solely focused on learning the first step of the UPS: body awareness.
- Learn to recognize the three types of body awareness: sensation, action, and urgency.

- Pause the screen time.
- This is the highly involved phase, where you'll be required to keep an eye out for your child's external cues throughout the day and help them connect those feelings to the need to go.
- When encountering resistance, utilize the parenting tools from Chapter 2, "The Big Picture."
- If you need to leave the house, it is okay to use a pull-up temporarily. Diapers do not define or limit their learning success.

8

Keep Going

Wait, I Thought I Was Done!

Over the next days, weeks, and months, you'll begin transitioning from the "highly involved" phase into the "occasionally involved" phase of potty training. This is the time where your child is able to identify their bodily sensations, and they're gradually increasing their lead time before they have to go. The pace of this transition is different for each kid. Some children may have everything click right away, and you can take a step back. But most kids need some level of support and continued teaching.

This is the phase where many parents get frustrated and lost. If they've been told that potty training can be finished within a long weekend, they are usually blindsided by the fact that they're still so involved in their child's toilet use. When issues arise, they get upset or feel ashamed, feeling like they (or their children) have failed a test.

But potty training isn't a binary—there's no one moment that can define whether a child is potty trained or not. Because who would get to draw that line? Obviously, just removing diapers doesn't make a child potty trained. But do they need to go an arbitrary amount of time without a miss to be officially deemed "potty trained"? If so, how long is that amount of time? A day? A week? A year? We all know that school-age kids still have occasional misses at times of stress or distraction. If that happens, does that mean your second grader is no longer potty trained? To take this thought experiment a step further: many birthing parents experience stress incontinence after pregnancy, labor, and delivery. If I pee when I sneeze, does that mean I'm not potty trained anymore?

Obviously, nobody is going to make that leap for older children or adults, so why do we put this same pressure on our toddlers? Instead of expecting them to wake up "potty trained" after just a few days of practice, we're going to continue supporting them through this learning process for a while.

Days Two and Three

On days two and three, you will continue building on the skills learned on day one, and it may seem like déjà vu all over again.

Or it may seem *harder*. Sometimes children perform wonderfully on day one because everything is new and exciting. Then, on day two or three, once the novelty wears off, kids will start to lose interest or even actively push back against the potty-training process.

If this happens to you, take a deep breath and remind yourself that it's totally normal. This is a marathon, not a sprint: you're teaching your child a fundamental skill they'll be using for the rest of their lives, it's okay if it doesn't happen overnight.

On day two, you'll be doing mostly the same thing as day one. We're still in the phase where we're trying to get your child to connect their body sensations with the need to sit on the potty. If your child is starting to do this, you can begin being a bit more flexible with the schedule, or even try to introduce undies if they're currently naked or commando.

On days two and three, you can also try and leave the house for longer without diapers. By day three, if you haven't done many outings, you may be going completely stir crazy. Though you can work toward longer outings, we're not quite ready to spend all day at the theme park yet. Instead, try a trip to your local playground (with your travel potty, wipes, and a change of clothes on hand). The idea is that we're stretching out the skills slowly and deliberately. This is not a "throw them in the deep end and see if they'll swim" situation—we're still working with gradual and incremental changes here.

Returning to School

Many children need to return to school after only a few days of potty training and this can be nerve wracking for parents! Most parents worry that their child's school will handle potty training in a way that hinders the process, or even causes them to forget what they've learned. Potty-training progress can seem so tenuous at times, and so many of us have been taught that one misstep can lead to a dreaded "regression."

First, I'd like to reassure you that, no matter how your child's school handles potty training, your kid will still make progress. Children are adaptable and understand the difference between how things are handled at school versus at home. The different environments cue kids to behave differently in each context. For instance, you may have a kid who refuses to clean up their own playroom at home, but happily puts away toys at school. A classic example is the child who will only nap at school, but stays awake all day when home.

Similarly, children are able to understand how different potty-training rules apply while at school. That said, there are some proactive steps you can take to try and make the potty-training experience more seamless for your child.

Most schools have an official potty-training policy. Inquire if they have one written up, or ask your kid's teachers for a rundown.

Some questions you should ask before your child returns to school:

- Are potty visits scheduled or based solely on a child's cues/asking to go?
- What language do you use to describe #1 and #2? (Or, could you adopt the language we use at home?)
- How are misses (a.k.a. "accidents") addressed?

- Will my child be put back in diapers after a certain number of misses? If so, how many, and when can they return to wearing underwear?
- What encouragement or praise does the school use when there is a success?
- How do you handle a child that asks for privacy when pooping?
- What is your wiping policy?
- What additional clothing or special gear do you require for potty training?
- How do you handle naps?

As an example, here is a typical policy among preschools I work with:

- Potty breaks are scheduled once per hour, or sooner if a child requests to go.
- We will use your family's preferred terms for elimination. Please list them for the teacher to learn.
- If a child has two pee accidents or one poop accident in a day, they will be put back in diapers for the remainder of the school day. They may return to school in underwear the following day.
- The school uses positive communication to encourage successful potty use. We will not be able to provide rewards for potty use.
- If a child needs privacy, a teacher will wait by the door to assist if needed.
- Our staff is licensed and trained to wipe and assist in the bathroom. We will encourage your child to make a first attempt at wiping, and then follow up to ensure they are clean.
- All children must have four full changes of clothes in their cubby. Please provide flushable wipes and two gallon-sized ziplock bags to contain soiled clothing.

- Children will be put in diapers for all naps. After ten consecutive days of waking up dry from naps, they may wear underwear at naptime.

If you find your school's policy differs significantly from your approach at home, all is not lost. Remember, you and the teachers are on the same team—after all, you already trust these educators to care for your precious child! There's no reason to create a contentious relationship because of a policy difference. Give them the benefit of the doubt, and assume their potty policy is based on their specific needs. After all, these teachers have many children to watch at once and need to customize their approach as a result.

In many cases, your child may find themselves back in diapers temporarily. This may happen because they hit a certain threshold of misses, or because the school requires a certain amount of "dry days" before removing diapers. Because of this, you should buy diapers with different patterns or colors so your child can distinguish between "school diapers" and "home diapers." This can be done during the rehearsal period to get a child used to the difference.

You may also want to ask your child's teachers how they interrupt playtime for a potty break. Many misses happen during deeply engaged play, and it can be difficult for teachers to break through. It can be helpful to share the external urgency signs your child exhibits when they need to go, whether it's their own specific style of potty dance or something more subtle. This can help cue a teacher into their need to go and begin drawing them away from play before there's a miss. And if your child's teacher is reporting frequent misses during play, ask them if you can share the section in Chapter 9 titled "Intense Focus on Play" to see if it inspires any solutions on their end.

In the end, even if your child's school takes a completely different approach, they may progress faster than a child who isn't attending school. At school, your child observes their already-potty-trained classmates having success on a daily basis. This type of peer-to-peer teaching is invaluable and often leads to greater success at home.

Heading Out and About

In Chapter 7, "It's Go Time," we discussed the approach for going out with a child in the highly involved phase of potty training. How you handle outings, travel, and activities will change as your child progresses into the occasionally involved stage.

When it comes to short, local outings, I recommend hoping for the best but preparing for the worst. Your child may stay dry the whole time and happily use whatever bathrooms are available, or they may have a giant miss that requires an outfit change or a return home. You can't always predict how your kid will fare, but you can at least be prepared for some common challenges.

If you travel mostly in your own car, you can keep a "miss kit" stashed away with your travel potty. This kit would include wet wipes, a complete change of clothes (including socks and shoes), an absorbent towel to soak up anything from the car seat cushions, hand sanitizer, and a resealable waterproof bag to hold soiled items.

When it comes to protecting your child's car seat, there's unfortunately only a few options available. Adding any after-market accessories to a car seat isn't safe unless it's specifically recommended by the manufacturer. That means you can't add a puppy pad or random "potty-training liner" you found online—these items haven't been crash tested and may compromise the safety of your car seat.

A few car seat manufacturers, like Britax and Diono, have their own official potty-seat liners that are approved for use. Other car seats, like some Clek models, may allow for a thin towel to be placed on the seat. You can find out your car seat's specifications by reading the manual and searching the FAQs on their website.

One more safety consideration is how you clean your car seat after a miss. Many parents don't realize that car seat cleaning must be done according to the manual, and some cleaning products can compromise the safety of your seat. Or you may opt for a car seat that has easily removable and machine-washable covers, like the Nuna Rava. A safe bet for cleaning up messes on the go is to have 100 percent water wipes on hand, and use the absorbent towel in your "miss kit" to soak up the pee. If your child has pooped in the seat, remove as much residue as possible before spot-cleaning with water.

For car rides longer than forty-five minutes, you may consider using a pull-up as a one-off solution. Some parents will put underwear on underneath a pull-up, hoping this will help their child feel the sensation of wetness while still protecting the car seat. If your child is okay with this, there's no harm in trying, but I wouldn't force it if all that extra bulk makes them uncomfortable.

If you decide to use a pull-up on a longer drive, consider it as insurance, not an excuse to skip bathroom breaks. Take regular breaks every two hours, even if your child seems perfectly content. Even if they don't need to use the bathroom, it's important for them to get out of their car seat at regular intervals. And if your child has a miss, don't let them sit in a wet diaper, make sure you pull over at the next bathroom and complete the steps of the Universal Potty Sequence.

The Potty Preview

When you're out and about, try a "potty preview." Whether it's a store, the park, or a friend's house, you can go check out the restroom right when you get there, even if you don't need to go. This is a great strategy for easing your child's discomfort with unfamiliar bathrooms. Once there, you can:

- Test out how loud the flush sounds. Even if you manage to postpone flushing your own toilet until your child is out of the stall, other people will be flushing around them.
- Similarly, test out any electric hand dryers to see how loud they blow. These can be even more scary than flushes for some kids. If they hate the sound, point out the paper towels, or show them how they can flap their hands to air dry them as an alternative.
- Carry sticky notes to put over the automatic-flush sensors. Toddlers are often too small to register on those sensors, so toilets will flush while they're still sitting. If you don't have a

sticky note, you can just cover it with your finger or possibly drape some toilet paper over it.

If your child is nervous about bathrooms, they'll likely be resistant to a potty preview. So you'll have to make it fun and casual, maybe saying, "I wonder if this bathroom is quieter or louder than ours at home? What's your guess?" Or you can peek in as you walk by and say, "oh my gosh, have you ever seen this many stalls? Check it out!" If you can get your child to even step into the bathroom, this proactive approach will allow your child to build a mental picture of what the bathroom will look, sound, and smell like. Then, if they need to go while you're out, you won't be introducing a brand-new environment to your child.

Air Travel

Ideally, you should have planned potty training to avoid any big travel within the first month or two. This suggestion is meant to give your child some time to make significant progress toward potty independence while still in their typical daily routine. Air travel often involves early mornings, late nights, and completely new environments for your child to adjust to. If you're also trying to balance learning a significant new skill like potty training, adding the tumult of travel can be a lot to ask of a small child.

But life happens, and you may find yourself needing to travel by plane before you feel your child is "ready." Maybe you got a late acceptance to a new preschool that requires potty training, but you already have your family vacation booked. Or, perhaps, a family member falls ill and you need to travel to be by their side.

While you can take much of the same advice as I gave for long car rides, there are a few unique considerations that make plane travel even trickier:

- *No floor potties:* Floor potties aren't going to fit in a plane bathroom and are inappropriate to use out in the main area of a plane.
- *Weird bathrooms:* Plane bathrooms are extremely small and difficult to navigate with an adult and a child. Plane toilets have

adult-sized seats and very loud flushes, which can be scary for children.

- *Missed opportunities:* You cannot leave your seat to potty at some points during the flight, like during turbulence or takeoff/landing. There may also be a long line for the one available toilet. So, even if a child indicates they have to go, they may not have the ability to get to the bathroom in time.
- *High-altitude effects:* The low air pressure can increase stomach bloating, which can make internal cues feel different and increase urgency. Also, the dry air can cause dehydration, which may cause your child to drink more fluids, leading to more urination.

There's no simple solution to many of these problems, but there are ways you can prepare for success. First, to combat the lack of a floor potty, invest in a foldable toddler toilet seat that you can keep in your carry-on. This will at least make the large toilet more comfortable for your child. If you can, before you take off, ask the flight attendant if you can do a "potty preview" (see the section in Chapter 9 titled "Fear" for more on how this works). If you think there's no way your child will sit on the plane's toilet, and you suspect they only need to pee, you can also have them use a disposable urinal bag while standing in the bathroom, and throw it away after they're done.

We can't control whether the fasten seat belt sign will be on the entire flight, or if your child will suddenly need to potty during takeoff. These are situations where your child will either stretch their skills and hold it until there's an opportunity, or they'll have a miss—there's not much you can do to intervene.

To try and prevent this kind of emergency, you should do a routine try immediately before boarding the plane. Most planes will let passengers use the bathrooms while parked at the gate, so you can also attempt a routine try before takeoff if time allows.

If your child expresses a need to go potty at an impossible time, you both may make the situation worse by getting anxious. In this scenario, try some calming techniques, like deep breaths, or even distraction. While I normally ask you to help your child be more in touch with their body's cues, in this particular scenario, distracting them by pointing out the clouds outside the window, or even showing them a screen, may help them relax enough to lessen their bladder pressure.

You know that feeling when a plane takes off and your ears start popping? That's a result of the lower air pressure you experience at high altitudes. Your ears pop because there's a tiny amount of trapped air inside your ear that expands (and leaves through your eustachian tube, hence the popping sound). But your ears aren't the only place with trapped air! Everyone's gut has some amount of gas inside, and if it can't escape via flatulence, it's going to cause bloating and pressure in your abdomen. If your kid is gassy, this bloating may translate into an increased need to go poop. If your child suddenly needs to go #2 when you reach cruising altitude, this phenomenon may be to blame. (Fun fact: this is why babies often have blowouts on takeoff.)

All of these factors can lead to a lot of stress when traveling. If you are unsure of your child's readiness to wait out long bathroom lines, or manage unexpected bloating, there is nothing wrong with using pull-ups while on the plane. You can explain to your child that these are only here in case they aren't allowed to go potty when they need to, or if the plane makes them feel funny and miss their own cues.

Whether or not you choose to use diapers for the flight, it's important to have a full change of clothes available—for both you and your child! Even if they have their own seat, many children will end up sitting on a parent's lap during a flight, so both of your clothes may become soiled. Or your clothes may become collateral damage as you carry your child to the bathroom after a miss. You should also have all the items from the "miss kit" that normally lives in your car. Don't forget a sealable, waterproof bag (a reusable wet bag or a zip-top plastic bag), so you can contain both the mess and the smell of soiled clothes.

A few other tips for long-distance travel while in the occasionally involved phase:

- If you didn't pack a small travel potty, pre-order a floor potty or seat insert to be used at your destination, and pick it up once you arrive.

- When choosing accommodations, prioritize options with laundry facilities. You may need to wash clothes in a hurry, and having a washer/dryer nearby can be quite handy.
- If staying with family, give them a quick rundown of the *Good to Go* method and your child's current status on their path toward potty independence. Ask them to avoid negative or pressuring language around your child, and make sure they understand that you're aiming for progress, not perfection.

Above all, give your child grace during these unusual situations. We've all witnessed adults who turn into the worst version of themselves during plane travel—busy airports and delayed flights are a pressure cooker for even the most serene traveler. Your child may be dealing with an out-of-whack schedule, different time zones, and harried parents. If your previously-potty-independent child suddenly starts having misses, chalk it up to the stress of travel and be kind and understanding. When you all return home, you can get back on track.

Potty Persuasion

Look, some kids will just never admit they have to go. It doesn't matter if you use all the most advanced parenting techniques, these kids will just dig in their heels and deny until it becomes an emergency (or a miss).

For kids like this, you'll need to be creative and playful. If you approach them in an accusatory or punitive tone, chastising them for not wanting to go potty, it's not only going to be ineffective but it will also undermine their bodily autonomy. And while we'd love for all children to be self-motivated from day one, there is usually a period of time where we need to persuade them to use the potty.

Following are a couple of techniques that may work.

"Prove Me Wrong"

Are you certain they need to go, but they insist they don't? Challenge them by saying, "okay, so prove me wrong! Show me!" Often a kid will race to the bathroom just to win the argument, and then discover they *do* have to pee, after all! This can be a win-win situation—if they don't pee, you can admit, "okay, you proved me wrong!" If they do pee, don't gloat about winning, but instead focus on the positive, "oh my gosh, I guess you did have to go! You must feel so relieved getting that pee in the potty!"

Surprise Pee

This technique has made its way around social media a few times, and it's a truly ingenious way to motivate resistant kids. Just ask, "Oh, do you think there's a surprise pee hidden in there? Let's go see!" If a pee does come out, you can exclaim, "Surprise! There is a pee! How exciting!" Kids may also enjoy yelling "surprise!" back at you. (This could work with poop as well, but may not be as quick!)

Aiming Games

If your child is standing to pee, you can throw a Cheerio into the bowl and see if they can hit the target. You can even buy colorful targets with trucks, dinosaurs, and animals that are printed on tissue paper—each trip to the toilet could be a mystery of "what animal showed up in the potty today?"

Race to the Potty/Fly to the Potty

Can they beat you to the potty? Or maybe they want to fly like a rocket ship? Anything to get them laughing en route!

The Not-Quite Five Senses

Ask your child to guess what their potty experience may be like. The idea is to utilize their senses to turn it into a game or mystery. You can come up with questions that have to do with the sense of touch, sound, or sight, but I would avoid anything with smell and taste, for obvious reasons!

You can ask:

- "Gosh, I wonder what color your pee is. Yellow or clear? Let's find out!"
- "Do you think you'll hear a waterfall or just a trickle when you pee?"
- "Do you think your pee will feel cold or warm coming out? Have you ever noticed?"

The Pitfalls of Pressure

While there's a time and place for potty persuasion, we need to strike a delicate balance between encouragement and pressure. If a child experiences too much external coercion to use the potty, there can be some serious consequences.

The biggest concern is that your child will develop a pattern of withholding. In later sections, we will go into more detail about poop withholding, constipation, and the resulting medical condition called encopresis. But one way to reduce your child's risk of these bowel issues is to keep pressure to a minimum. Try to keep the tone light, take misses in stride, and adapt your approach to match your child's personality.

Even if your kid doesn't develop withholding, too much pressure may strain your parent-child dynamic and cause problems outside of potty training. My goal is to always keep your bond at front of mind and make sure you prioritize maintaining a collaborative and loving relationship with your child. If this means taking a break from potty training, so be it.

Advanced Schedule

Here's a sample daily schedule for a kid in the occasionally involved stage of potty training. This applies to children who have gone a few days without a miss, and have clearly started to connect their body's cues to the need to go!

Again, for the sake of a sample schedule I am going to pack it with all kinds of things that would normally be spread across many days. I want to give you examples of lots of different types of situations, so you can feel prepared.

7:00 a.m.—Rise and Shine!

- Start the day with some cuddles and encouragement. Let them know that they are doing a great job of listening to their body.
- Ask them to pat their diaper. Does it feel full? Gushy with pee?
  - If yes, then walk over to the bathroom together to take it off and see what's inside. Invite them to sit on the potty and see if there are any surprise pee sprinkles left in their bladder—this is a routine try.
  - If their diaper is dry, then walk them over to the bathroom and say, "Your body has been holding your pee all night! Time to let it out."
- Fully dress them today with underwear, loose-fitting clothing, or any clothing that gives them easy access!

7:30 a.m.—Breakfast Time

- Have your breakfast as normal—there's no need to line the seat today since they will be dressed.
- Talk about how you will be spending your day:
  - "Today we will be going for a car ride to see how it feels listening to your body while we are driving." Modify this if you are walking or taking public transit.
  - "Every time before we go out, we try to go potty first. So do I!" Use the special phrase that you came up with for a routine try.

8:00 a.m.—Going Out

- Get ready to go out. For this example, let's say you are going to the playground.
- Make sure your "miss kit" is stocked and ready to go, and the travel potty is with you.
- While you're out, you may revert to using more prompting to avoid a miss while away from home.
- When you get to the park always start with the potty preview:
  - "Let's go see what the bathrooms here are like."
  - Maybe even listen for someone to flush, or flush a toilet yourself to see how loud it is.
- Have fun playing at the park and wait to see if your child is giving any cues or wants to try and use the bathroom there.
- If they reject that bathroom, no problem, that is what the travel potty is for!
- In case you encounter some resistance, here is an example of how to handle it:

Parent: "You have been playing for a while now and I am guessing there might be some pee that wants to come out?"
Child: "No, I don't need to go!"
Parent: "I can walk with you and we can try together, or I can pick you up and carry you to the potty?"
Child: "NO! I want to play!"
Parent: "I hear you, you really still want to play. I am worried that your bladder is full and the best way to check is to sit on the potty and see if anything comes out. Can you tell me, what do I want?"
Child: "You want me to check."
Parent: "Yes, that's right. I want you to check, and you want to still play. What should we do?"
Child: "Still plaaaayyy!"

Parent: "How about I put the little potty under your bottom to see if a surprise pee comes out and then you can still play right after. Deal?"
Child: "Okay."
Parent: "Let's shake on it."
(Parent and child shake hands.)
Parent: "Okay, here's the little potty. I am so curious to see what happens. What do you think is going to happen?"

- Attempt another routine try before you leave the park, whether it's at the park bathroom or in the travel potty.
- Head home after your routine try.
- If your child didn't pee before you left the park (even though they tried) and didn't pee on the car ride, then say, "We just got home. Let's give it a try!"

10:00 a.m.—Snack

- Refuel after your park outing! Consider including fresh fruits and berries in your child's snack, as they contain fiber and water that will help with pottying!

10:30 a.m.—Emotional Hygiene Practice

- Spend a few minutes in your cozy corner practicing another emotional-regulation technique (see Chapter 2, "The Big Picture").

10:30 a.m.—Planned Activity/Class

- Maybe your child has a gymnastics or music class. Bring your "miss kit" to this activity!
- When you arrive, this is another good opportunity for a potty preview. It will help a child to know exactly where the potty is so they can try and get there in time.

- Tell the teachers that your child has recently potty trained and may need to be excused during class. Explain to your kid that it's okay to take a break anytime, nobody will be upset with them if they ask to leave class to potty.

- If there are older children there, you can discreetly point out when children are using the bathroom on their own and say something like "So and so knows how to listen to their body and use the potty, too!"

- If you are sitting on the sidelines, still keep an eye out for some of their body cues (like seeing them crouch in a corner). You may need to physically go in to the class to help your child navigate to the potty.

- When class is over, if they haven't peed since you've left home, suggest a routine try before you leave. If you arrived in your own car, you can also offer the travel potty.

12:00 p.m.—Lunch

- Chat about the day and how they handled their travel and outings.

- If they stayed dry, highlight their choices to engage in routine tries and/or follow their cues and go right away.

- If there were misses, this is a chance for reflection. Ask "what do you think we could have done differently to avoid the miss?" Your child may have some good ideas, like trying a routine try during the class water break.

12:30 p.m.—Getting Ready for Nap

- It's time for another routine try before getting into sleep diapers.

- Encourage them to linger on the potty by reading them a book or telling them a story. After meals is a common time for poops!

1:00 p.m.—Naptime

- Get your child settled in for a nap in their sleep diaper.

2:30 p.m.—Wake Up and Potty Check

- As soon as they wake, ask them to squeeze their diaper. "Did pee come out while you were asleep?" If yes, go to the bathroom to complete the rest of the Universal Potty Sequence.
- If not, say, "Wow, I bet there is some pee ready to come out now! Let's go!"

3:00 p.m.—Snack Time

- "I bet you're thirsty and hungry after that nap! We need to eat and drink so our bodies can be fueled and hydrated so we can keep playing!"

4:00 p.m.—Afternoon Play

- Follow their lead for afternoon playtime activities.
- Keep an eye out for their cues, but you don't need to prompt like you did during outings. While at home, this is a safe space for them to start testing their ability to self-motivate and sense body cues.

5:30 p.m.—Dinner Prep

- This will be the time of the day that you will shift your highly involved focus off of your child and onto another task.
- If you are comfortable with screen time, then this is a good time to see how it goes. "I wonder if you can listen to your body and watch a show at the same time? Let's try. We can always pause the show if you have the pee feeling and I will come right away!"

- If you're not doing screen time, you can either keep them close and get them involved with the cooking, or let them play independently and see how they manage their sensation cues.

6:00 p.m.—Dinner Time

- Same as all the other mealtimes!
- While having dinner, engage in conversation about "How was it going to the park today?"

6:30 p.m.—Bath Time

- While the water is running, have your child sit on the potty to try and prevent a bath pee! Also, remember that meals can prompt a poop, so this is a good opportunity to linger.
- Even children who are well past potty training will occasionally pee in the bath. Don't make a big deal out of it (it's not a health issue), but casually say "next time let's get that pee in the potty instead!" You don't want to turn bathtime pees into a fun game.
- After bath, you can try a little naked time without worry, since they're now on a roll!

7:00 p.m.—Wind-Down and Bedtime Routine

- Do your regular wind-down routine before putting on their nighttime diaper. We want to give them a chance for a final potty before bed without relying on their sleep diaper.
- Before tuck in, say, "I always try to pee right before going to sleep, do you want to try?"

8:00 p.m.—Going to Sleep

- Put on their sleep diaper as the final step.
- Review the day together. Share what progress you saw, listen to what thoughts your child has, and think about tomorrow.

Once they're asleep, it's time for YOU to relax! Cheers!

Chapter in Review

- After the day one novelty wears off, you might encounter some unexpected curveballs.
- If attending daycare or preschool, familiarize yourself with their potty policy.
- Remember these potty-persuasion tricks: "prove me wrong," surprise pee, aiming games, races, and the five senses game.
- Use the "reinforce" step of the Values-Centered Parenting without turning it into pressure. Simply notice and mention the effort and steps they make in their learning journey.
- Create a "miss kit" for car rides or longer outings.
- When going out, use "potty previews" for unfamiliar bathrooms.
- Check out the advanced schedule to see what a packed day can look like diaper free.

9

Expect the Unexpected

What's YOUR Challenge?

Something that has always bothered me about existing potty-training methods is that they treat the tricky issues that arise as "problems" that need to be solved. The implication is pretty accusatory, implying that if you had just done everything right, your child wouldn't be having so many "problems" with using the potty.

This doesn't take into account the fact that the "problems" you face are not separate from potty training, but actually integrated into the process. Your child is wonderfully unique and may laugh in the face of our best-laid plans. So, if you're coming to this chapter in a panic, thinking you've done something wrong, I'm here to absolve you. Anyone taking the time to read this book obviously cares deeply about their children and wants to be the best parent possible. You're doing great.

Instead of going through a laundry list of "problems" to solve, I like to take a more systematic approach. My goal is to help you find the root cause of any challenge you're facing and try and find a creative and supportive way to support your child through it, rather than just suggest a quick-fix solution.

This is all getting esoteric, so let's talk about a real example.

Bedtime Distraction?

A client came to me because their three-year-old, Lucas, was having frequent pee misses, even though he had been diaper free for almost six months. When I asked if there was any pattern, in timing or activities, they said it often happened while he played quietly before bed, while they were in the kitchen cleaning up after dinner. Lucas would appear in the kitchen with wet jammies night after night.

On first blush, this seems like a classic challenge of a kid being too engrossed in play, and they should work to break the play spell.

But then I asked if it happens at other playtimes, and they said Lucas was fine during the day, this only happened at night. Could it still be a focus issue, where he was just tired and missing out on body cues at night?

I asked them to neglect the dishes for a bit so they could sit with Lucas while he played and observe exactly what happened. That night, the mom sat in the bedroom with Lucas while he played before bed. When she spotted Lucas wiggling his butt, she prepared herself for a struggle to pull him away from his toys. "Lucas, I see you doing the pee-pee dance, let's try to potty."

But it wasn't a challenge to get him to stop playing. He looked up and said, "but mommy, it so dark!" The mom realized that the hallway and bathroom lights were switched off. Lucas wasn't too engrossed in play to go potty, he was scared.

They had originally potty trained in the summer, when the sun set well after Lucas's bedtime. As the days shortened, and then daylight savings time reverted, Lucas was suddenly expected to take himself to the potty in the dark.

The parents got some bright nightlights for the hallway and got in the habit of turning the bathroom light on right after dinner. I also recommended they move a floor potty into Lucas's room temporarily, to give him a safe option while he overcomes his fear.

The Issue Behind the Issue

Finding the root cause of a potty-training challenge is crucial if you're going to overcome it. Even when it seems obvious, you should approach each issue with curiosity. Don't be quick to jump to conclusions, or make judgments about your kid's intentions.

Most potty challenges can be boiled down to one of these root causes:

- Fear
- Performance anxiety
- Intense focus on play
- Distraction
- Resistance and defiance
- Indifference
- Poop problems
- Physical lack of sensation awareness

As you encounter difficulties with your child, ask yourself if any of these things could explain the issue.

Fear

Some fears can seem irrational to adults, but they are all too real for a small child. Bathrooms can be scary places for kids. From a sensory perspective, bathrooms are full of horrors. They can be dark, smelly, and noisy. We are all born with an instinctual fear of loud noises, and it's only natural that kids get startled by them. Public bathrooms are the worst offenders (public park bathrooms are a real test for even the bravest child), but even the home bathroom can bring up scary feelings for kids. For instance, some children's innate fear of heights is triggered by sitting on an adult-sized toilet.

If you suspect your child's potty issues stem from fear, your goal should be to give them tools and techniques to start coping with their fear. Please avoid pressure tactics like labeling them ("you're a big girl now"), threatening consequences ("if you don't use the potty, we can't go to the toy store"), or comparing them to peers ("Liam goes all by himself!"). Even if well-intentioned, this kind of motivation is very stressful for a child trying to overcome a fear.

Instead, we want to provide compassionate support. Here are a few techniques to try at home:

- Consider using a seat insert to make the bowl opening smaller. This will help with a child who is afraid of falling.
- If the seat insert isn't enough, your child can sit backward, straddling the bowl and resting their arms on the tank. This can also be an opportunity to be silly, which should lighten the mood and create positive associations with the bathroom.
- With small children, you can even "ride tandem" with them, where you straddle the potty and they sit in front of you, as though you're both on a motorcycle.
- Pair potty time with a fun activity, like singing a silly song, reading a book, or drawing on an erasable tablet.
- Use scented products to mask unpleasant odors. You can use a toilet-bowl spray like Poo-Pourri, or have a plug-in diffuser going at all times.
- If the noise of a bathroom fan or flushing is too much, you can keep some noise-canceling headphones (like a kid would wear to a concert) in the bathroom.

When your child doesn't need to potty, you can work on the following skills:

- Practice teaching your child how to pinch their nose to block out bad scents.
- Demonstrate how covering your ears blocks out a lot of scary noises. You can find sound effects libraries on most music streaming services—play ambulance sirens, jackhammering sounds, and other loud noises and ask your kid to see how quiet they can make them by covering their own ears.
- Develop a mantra to help your child be brave in the future. I like "I am scared, but I am safe. I can do scary things."

Performance Anxiety

Performance anxiety may present as fear, but the root cause is internal instead of external. While fearful children are scared of the environment and conditions of the bathroom, kids with performance anxiety are scared of their own bodily functions.

Some children find it very distressing to know that their pee and poop are leaving their bodies. Subconsciously, they may think that they're flushing away a body part—after all, moments before, it *was* inside their body!

For kids like this, you want to start by creating a calm environment in the bathroom. Running the sink can create soothing white noise while also reminding them of a stream of water. You could also play calming music at a low volume, or go so far as to light a candle and dim the lights.

It can take some time to get them comfortable, so make sure there's a basket nearby with books and toys that will facilitate some quiet, independent play.

Whether or not they successfully use the potty, use descriptive praise to acknowledge their efforts. Don't go over the top with enthusiasm, as cheering "Good job!" paired with a high-five can be misconstrued as pressure. Instead, keep your tone measured, upbeat, and factual. You could say:

- "You sat on the potty and tried, that was brave."
- "You used the step stool and balanced on the potty."
- "You pushed your pants down all by yourself."
- "You listened to your body."

Sometimes, the root cause of performance anxiety can be perfectionism. A perfectionist kid may act helpless or defeated, because if they can't do something just right, why bother trying at all? If you suspect your child may have perfectionist tendencies, the best place to start is by leaning heavily on the modeling portion of the Values-Centered Parenting tool. If the core value is "progress, not perfection," you can start modeling the value of trying something repeatedly and not being perfect all the time. For instance, "Oh, this parking spot is so hard to get into, our car is all crooked! I'm going to pull back and keep trying until I get in straight." When children see that we can mess up and it's not the end of the world, they're more likely to be willing to try a new skill.

Intense Focus on Play

If your child struggles to pause their playtime in order to go potty, you're not alone. This is a very common challenge with children, and it can be very difficult to break the spell of engrossing play.

If your child has misses while playing, I'd first investigate whether it's happening at other times as well. We want to rule out other causes, like an actual lack of body awareness or some kind of health issue. But if it's mostly happening when they're laser-focused on their play, it's safe to assume that their body-awareness cues are just having trouble breaking through.

Until they get more practice recognizing these internal cues, you will need to act as their external reminder in the interim. When your child is playing, keep in mind when they've last gone potty and what their usual rhythm is. If you notice any cues, like the potty dance, or know it's past their usual time to go, you can try a few things to make the transition away from playtime smoother:

- Get on their level. Before you start talking, break their concentration with some physical touch, like a hand on their arm. Then say, "It's been a while since you went potty. Is your body giving you any clues?"
- If you know they have to go, simply say, "potty time!" Keep it short and sweet. Maintain gentle physical touch as you guide them toward the bathroom.
- Reassure them that they can come right back to their toys. "It looks like you're having so much fun, this will be quick and we'll get right back to playing."
- If they don't want to leave their toys, you can fold a piece of paper in half and create a simple sign that says "SAVE." Ceremoniously place this over their activity and say, "this is the official 'save' sign, so your toys aren't going anywhere."
- If siblings or other kids are around, create a safe space for your child to stash their toys while they're gone.

Distraction

Misses that happen due to distraction are often similar to the play-based challenge we just talked about. The main difference is that the distraction is something external and out of the child's control that's pulling their focus.

The most common distraction scenario is a miss that happens while watching television. Many children can get completely sucked into screen time, whether it's a movie, show, or game, and this will interrupt their ability to notice their own body's cues. Unlike playing with toys, which is something a child can choose to stop at any time, a screen is often out of their control. Kids aren't often in charge of whether a screen is on or off—for example, if a parent is watching sports, or if you're out at a restaurant that has TVs.

But screen time isn't the only distraction. Some children may become distracted by siblings (you can't turn off your brother!), house guests, or even listening to their teacher give a lesson.

The techniques for breaking this pattern are going to be similar to the advice given in the previous section. The parent will need to keep an eye on the clock and prompt a potty break if it's been long enough or the child is showing any cues. Get down on their level, create physical touch, and use simple instructions to guide them to the bathroom. If you can, pause the television so your child doesn't have a fear of missing out. If you can't pause the distraction, validate their worry about missing something, but remind your child that the potty break will be quick. You can also move the floor potty into the room so they have a better chance of catching a pee or poo, even with the distraction nearby.

If possible, take a break from screen time for a few days. This will allow your child to build up some more experience connecting their body's sensations to the need to go potty, without the intense distraction of their favorite show. If screen time is necessary, there's no judgment here—it's an effective tool for caregivers to get some breathing room in their days. If that's the case, just build in a routine try before the screen turns on. You can say, "I've noticed you have trouble noticing how your body feels while the TV is on. Let's try to potty beforehand, so that's not a problem." Set a boundary that the screen doesn't get turned on without a routine try.

JUST HIDE THE REMOTE

The second time we tried potty training Auggie, it was going much better than the first go-around. He was a year older and was much more adept at picking up on his body's cues. On days one and two, he had almost no misses. We were so excited!

Then, on day three, things went sideways. Because the first couple of days were such a success, we got right back into our normal routine on day three without much trepidation. And that included some quality time with the television.

Though it was a controversial topic among other toddler parents, screen time was a normal part of Auggie's life. At first I was sheepish about his watching habits, not wanting to admit that he was watching television at all. But I eventually realized that appreciating visual storytelling is a core family value, and also part of his DNA. His dad is a television writer, and we all love movies. And though he wasn't parked in front of the TV all day, he did watch a little bit every day.

So, with his early success with potty training, I didn't even think twice about turning on the TV.

But then he had a miss while sitting on the couch.

And another the next day.

And then another later that evening.

We all started to get frustrated; what had happened? It didn't take long to connect the dots: all his misses were while he was watching TV. I realized he was so engrossed in his show that he just didn't recognize his need to pee.

So, we told Auggie that we were turning the TV off for a few days. He was not at all pleased with this decision, and there was a lot of protesting. I had the foresight to make sure he knew this wasn't an issue of discipline—I didn't want him to think we were being punitive because he had a miss. I explained to him, "honey, I know you love watching TV, I do, too. But it's just too distracting and it's blocking you from listening to your own body. Once we go two days without a miss, we can try to watch TV again."

> I hope he understood that this wasn't a punishment, but it's possible he still thought we were being big meanies. But the system worked! Whether he was simply motivated to get back to his favorite shows or the extra days helped shore up his body-awareness skills, he stayed dry for the rest of the week, and we were able to reintroduce screen time without any more misses.

Resistance and Defiance

Do you have a child who resists all routine tries and hates reminders? Do they intentionally hold their pee during a bathroom stop just to prove you wrong? Maybe they actively push back on requests, regardless of the topic?

Kids like this can be especially challenging for parents. They value freedom and choice, but resist assignments or routines. Many times, we have no choice but to force our kids to complete tasks. But for these kinds of kids, any type of request is met with knee-jerk resistance. If they get a whiff of any hint of expectation, *they* will push back. Sometimes, they'll even stop doing something they want to do because there's an outer expectation.

If you have a child like this, you're not alone. Toddlers are notorious for their defiant personalities (everyone has heard of the "terrible twos"), and some level of resistance is going to be expected. However, if your child consistently pushes back on every single request, it could be an early sign of something called oppositional defiant disorder (ODD). ODD is very common—some estimates say more than one in ten children will get this diagnosis. It's difficult to identify ODD in small children, but parents report children who have persistent tantrums, resistance to rules, defiance to all requests (even for things they like), and an unwillingness to compromise. If you suspect your child may have some signs of ODD, the book *The Explosive Child* by Ross W. Greene, PhD, has excellent advice to help parents with a child who is resistant to authority in any form.

In this section, we will address more run-of-the-mill defiance, where the resistant behaviors happen occasionally, but not consistently.

If you're running into this kind of defiant behavior, the first approach would be to employ natural and logical consequences for your child.

When it comes to potty training, we should start with the "I've noticed" and problem-framing sequence, as introduced in Chapter 2, "The Big Picture."

"I've noticed that it's hard for you to stop playing to go potty. I wonder if you can think of a way to pause your play to go potty?"

It's possible your child may have a solution, or you can suggest one in an open-ended way: "What if we put your toys on a high shelf so nobody else will take them while you're gone?"

If that works, great! But if your child still resists, it's time to employ natural and logical consequences. A few examples:

- Natural consequence: "If you don't use the potty, you'll have a miss. Your pants will be wet, and we'll have to stop whatever we're doing to clean up."

- Logical consequence: "If you don't use the potty, you'll have a miss and I will need to put the toys aways for a little while so you can focus."

- Natural consequence: "If you have another miss, you will be all wet and need a bath."

- Logical consequence: "If you have another miss, you will need to wear your diapers again and not your underwear."

For many kids, these natural and logical consequences are enough. It will likely take repetition and consistency, but they will be able to predict how their choices affect an outcome, and act accordingly.

Indifference

No matter how much time and effort you put into the rehearsal period, there are some children who just don't show any interest in using the potty. For whatever reason, these kids lack the intrinsic motivation to put effort into this milestone. This isn't a reflection on your ability to teach, but instead an insight on how they learn. In these cases, you may need to resort to some illogical consequences. A highly resistant child may need a rewards system that externalizes the motivation, as they will be unlikely to be self-motivated to use the potty.

The nerdy child development term for this is additive reinforcement, though many parents half-jokingly call it "the bribery method."

This may be the most controversial topic in potty training: is it okay to give my child rewards for using the potty? Some people use sticker charts, while others offer small toys or sweet treats as a reward for successful pees and poops in the potty.

I always recommend starting potty training *without* the use of any external incentives. Many children don't require any kind of bribe to successfully potty train, so there's no reason to set the precedent of giving rewards if it's not necessary. However, if your child is very resistant and all other tactics aren't working out, it's okay to use this as additive reinforcement. While incentives create a dependency on external validation, they are sometimes necessary and can be helpful if set up properly.

If your child seems to have no internal drive to potty train, or they continue to be resistant after multiple days, this may be your best bet.

The flip side of this coin is subtractive reinforcement, where your child loses something for an undesired behavior. For example, your child gets to watch TV every evening for thirty minutes, unless they have a miss. This is harder to set up than an additive reinforcement system, as it requires your child to connect not doing something with a reward. Another example of subtractive reinforcement would be if you have a sticker chart for successfully using the toilet—if your child has a miss, they don't get a sticker.

If you decide to use rewards, it's important to establish that it's only a short-term fix! You should have a tapering plan from the start. For instance, you'll tell your child, "For the first week, you'll get a sticker every time you use the potty. But after that, we'll only get a sticker every other time." By gradually reducing the frequency of the rewards as your child becomes more consistent, you'll lessen their need for external validation and give yourself an off-ramp from the potty-reward cycle.

Poop Problems

Has your child mastered peeing, but refuses to poop in the potty? This is a very common issue, and possibly the most frustrating challenge for potty-training parents.

The number one rule for kids who refuse to poop in a potty: allow them to poop however they are comfortable. For many kids, this means they'll need a diaper or pull-up just for a daily poop. No, this will not "derail" potty training, or confuse your child. I want you to hear this and take it to heart: it is absolutely fine for your child to poop in a diaper if it's the only way they'll go.

The reason I'm hammering this in is because we want to do everything in our power to avoid constipation. The more a child withholds, the more they run the risk of chronic constipation. Constipation is the enemy of potty training, and it will do more to delay potty independence than inconsistent use of diapers.

Constipation is a sneaky issue in children. It doesn't always present as hard stool or going many days without pooping. In fact, if a child has chronic constipation, it may look like frequent diarrhea, which can be confusing for parents and delay a proper diagnosis.

To understand all this, I need to go into a little anatomy lesson. When food leaves the stomach, it enters the small intestine, where it is further broken down and turned into liquid. Then, this liquid enters the large intestine (a.k.a. the colon), where the water is absorbed and a solid poop begins to form. The poop bolus then enters the rectum, which is basically the waiting room. Once that poop is hanging out, you feel it pushing on your anus and know it's time to go #2. Once on the toilet, you relax your muscles and let the poop out.

However, if you keep holding it in, water continues to be removed from the poop, making it harder and more compact. This kind of poop can be painful on the way out. If a child has a hard and painful poop, they may start associating the action with pain and become scared of pooping. But this is a vicious cycle, because then more poop backs up in the waiting room and gets harder in the process. This stretches their rectum out like a balloon, causing a large backup of hard, dry poop to stay put in their colon. At this point, the liquid poop from higher up in the colon can sneak its way around the existing constipation and come out as diarrhea. What's worse, due to the stretched-out rectum, a child often loses the ability to feel poop urgency and will soil themselves without even realizing it. This is a symptom called encopresis and can be very embarrassing for parents and children alike.

If you're reading this and you recognize these symptoms in your child, it's time to go to your doctor. Your child's pediatrician or gastroenterologist can prescribe medicine to help soften the existing poop and give you guidance on how to help your child's colon return to normal.

Your child likely isn't at this point yet, but it is helpful to know what's at stake with extended withholding. The above scenario is exactly why I recommend you allow your child to poop in diapers if needed—we'd rather take longer to master pooping in the potty than develop chronic constipation or encopresis.

Now, if your child isn't exhibiting signs of serious constipation, but is still refusing to poop in the potty, there are a few ways we can help gently encourage them to try. First, make sure they are already squatting to poop. If this isn't happening yet, return to the pooping posture section in Chapter 5 and apply the solutions found there.

Once you've confirmed your child is squatting, build in a routine try immediately after meals. There's something called the "gastrocolic reflex," which is just a fancy way of saying we usually have to poop after we eat. (You may remember this phenomenon happening with your kids as small babies, but it continues throughout our lives!) Make the bathroom or floor potty as peaceful and calm as possible and have lots of toys and books available to allow your child to sit as long as they need.

If your child has mild constipation (hard poops or withholding for less than three days), you can try some at-home remedies to help soften their stool and make it easier to pass.

Some constipation can be addressed by modifying your child's diet. An easy thing to remember is "Eat your Ps, don't be a BRAT." (This is a mnemonic just for you, please don't actually call your child a brat!) Common "P" foods that soften poop include pears, plums, peaches, prunes/prune juice, pineapple, and papaya. The BRAT diet refers to bananas, rice, applesauce, and toast, which can make constipation worse. You may also consider removing cow's milk from your child's diet to see if it has an effect—lactose intolerance is a common cause of constipation.

You can also utilize yoga and gentle massage to help relieve stress and improve bowel motility. Some poses that may help are belly breathing, butterfly pose, cat-cow stretch, child's pose, frog pose (including some jumps if you want), torso twists, and happy baby. While I've been practicing yoga for years, you'll be better off finding online video demonstrations of all these poses rather than having me explain each one!

You can also gently massage your child's belly by moving your hands in a clockwise motion across their abdomen. Another fun way to do a belly massage is to have your child lie flat on their back while you face them and hold their ankles. Then gently push their knees up to their chest and rotate them around. Using a microwaveable weighted plushie as a heating pad can also provide comforting pressure and warmth to the stomach.

If your child has experienced pain while pooping, they may have developed a fear around the potty. You can consult the above section about fear and add in some of the anti-constipation foods to make sure they don't have future hard poops. If they continue to experience pain, even with soft stools, you should consult your pediatrician to rule out an anal fissure, hemorrhoids, or other painful problem.

And finally, if your child will poop in the potty at home, but not while out and about, that's nothing to worry about. Many adults have the same quirk! It's so common there's actually a term for it: "shy bowel" or parcopresis. With gentle reassurance and modeling, your child will hopefully outgrow this issue in time. But even if they don't, most people can live normal lives while only pooping at home, and this shouldn't become an issue that causes power struggles between you and your child.

Physical Lack of Sensation Awareness

After the first phase of potty training, you may notice your child is still having a lot of misses. After reading through all these common challenges, and trying all the techniques, you are still cleaning up messes every day.

In this case, I suspect your child still doesn't have the fundamental body-sensation awareness to self-initiate to go potty. This is a common issue when parents or preschool teachers take kids to the potty at predefined intervals, usually between every forty-five minutes to an hour. While this approach can be useful for a very short time, if it continues past a few days it can provide a false sense of success. Your kid will have learned how to physically use the potty—they release pee or poop whenever someone sits them down on it—but they've never connected their body cues to the need to go in the first place.

These kids will be labeled as "potty trained" solely because they are using a toilet, but they still haven't learned step one of the Universal Potty Sequence. Then, when the timed reminders go away, these children start having misses and are chastised for "regressing."

Some kids who show signs of a lack of sensation awareness may respond to rewards and incentives. Check out the "Indifference" section above to see if creating some kind of additive reinforcement external rewards system may be a good option for your child. However, I would avoid using subtractive reinforcement—we don't want your child to feel punished for something that may still be entirely out of their developmental control. The rewards are simply meant to provide some added positive reinforcement to help your child get past the "notice the sensation" step.

However, you may notice your child still has no ability to connect their sensation to the need to go potty. If this describes your child, you'll likely need to take a break and put diapers back on while you go back and work on the fundamentals. If the issue wasn't timed tries, but your child is still having trouble with sensation awareness, there could be a few causes. First, you may have just started potty training too soon, and your toddler needs more time to mature. Or, your child may have a physical or developmental issue that's interfering with their ability to learn this step. For now, take a break from potty training to investigate the root cause. You can read the following section, "A Potty Pause," to learn exactly how to navigate that process.

Bedtime Delays and Overnight Challenges

Stalling Tactics

Potty training can breathe new life into a familiar parenting challenge: bedtime stalling. By the time you have a toddler, you've probably experienced the old classics: "one more kiss," "one more story," "I need a drink of water." But now you might hear, "I have to go potty!" And suddenly, you're stuck wondering: Is this a real need or a clever delay tactic?

Obviously, we want to believe our children when they say they need to go potty, but kids are very attuned to how we react. When you're still in the highly involved phase of potty training, your instinct will be to jump to attention any time your child says they need to go, even if they're already tucked in. This cause and effect is not lost on your child, and they may use it to their advantage to push their bedtime later and later.

To preempt this, include a potty attempt in their routine as close as possible to their actual bedtime. This final routine try should happen right before the lights go out and their body begins to settle into sleep.

If your child insists they need to go after lights out, keep it a low-stimulation event. Bring in the floor potty and let them sit briefly, with lights low and no added conversation or distraction. This helps them stay connected to the sleepy bedtime state rather than starting the whole wind-down process over again. You can use wipes to "wash" their hands and tuck them right back into bed.

Trust your instincts. If your gut says it's a stall tactic and not a true urge, you can gently say: "We already tried, remember? If your body still has to go in the morning, we'll go right when you wake up. Your job right now is to rest your body so it can do a great job tomorrow."

If you suspect what they're really seeking is you, offer a moment of connection—rub their back, hum a lullaby, or give a final squeeze—without re-opening the whole bedtime process and linking it to a phantom potty urge.

Don't forget, most kids will still be in nighttime diapers at this stage, so there's not a lot at stake. If they don't use the potty, but end up peeing while asleep, it will be caught in their pull-up.

If these stall tactics begin happening every night, it's okay to point it out with kindness and a solution. Here are some sample scripts:

> "I've noticed that you usually ask to go potty again after we're all tucked in. Sometimes that means you're not quite ready to say goodnight yet. Let's practice listening to your body during our bedtime potty time, and if you need to go more in the morning, we always will."
>
> "Hmm, your body already had a chance to try, and now it's time to rest. Sometimes when it's hard to say goodnight, our brain thinks of all kinds of things to do—like going potty again. Let's trust that your body will tell us in the morning if it still needs to go, and right now your job is to get cozy and rest."

You may be concerned that this will derail the potty-training process, but it's not something I worry about. In fact, it's just another opportunity to reinforce body awareness in a low-pressure way. You can say something like, "Let's check—press right here on your belly and see if it's really a pee feeling, or maybe you just wanted a hug." This keeps the focus on listening to their body, while also honoring their emotional need in the moment.

With continued daytime practice, they'll grow stronger in recognizing real cues. And at night, if you consistently redirect toward comfort instead of starting the whole bedtime routine over, they'll learn to ask for what they truly need without the potty detour.

Middle-of-the-Night Wakings

If your child starts waking in the middle of the night to go potty, you'll need to do a little detective work to figure out the root cause. Do they really need to pee or does nothing come out when you try? And is this happening like clockwork at the same time every night, or is it more irregular?

When They Truly Need to Go

It may not seem like it, but if your child is waking up to go to the bathroom at 2:00 a.m. and they successfully use the potty, this is good news! This means their body is starting to make the connection between full bladder signals and waking up rather than just going in their sleep diaper. This is a major developmental step and a sign that they may be getting closer to outgrowing their sleep diapers. But there are a few things you can do to make it easier on you:

- Start offering more fluids earlier in the day and gradually taper off in the evening. A good rule of thumb is to reduce liquids about 1–1.5 hours before bedtime.

- Make sure their routine try is as close to bedtime as possible. You may need to rearrange the order of their bedtime routine to accommodate this.

- Try a dream pee by gently waking your child approximately two to three hours after they have fallen asleep (or right before you hit the hay). Remember to use the floor potty and keep it low stimulation, just like you would for a bedtime-stalling try. (For more on this topic, see "To Dream Pee or Not to Dream Pee?" in Chapter 10, "Now We're Cruising.")

If this is happening at the same time every night, move on to the techniques found in the next section, "When It's Like Clockwork."

When It's Like Clockwork

If your child is waking at the same time every night to go pee, we need to work on resetting their internal clock. In these cases, their body has become programmed to wake up, even if they may not need to go at all. Adults experience the same phenomenon—if your alarm wakes you up at 6:00 a.m. every weekday, you may find your eyes open at the crack of dawn on Saturdays. We all have an internal clock, and when our brains get into a pattern, sometimes that pattern persists, even when it's not needed.

Children cycle through periods of deep and light sleep throughout the night. When it comes to predictable nighttime wakings, your child is likely hitting a light sleep phase at the same time every night. At this point in sleep, they have more body awareness and may notice the pressure in their bladder which, in turn, makes them wake up fully and call out to you. And now you're in a familiar chicken-and-egg conundrum: It's very difficult for you to discern whether they woke up because they have to pee or if they have to pee just because they woke up.

To attempt to break this cycle, you'll need to address two separate systems: bladder and brain.

First, let's ensure their bladder is set up for success. Limit late-in-the-day fluid intake and attempt a low-stimulation dream pee as described in the previous section.

Second, we need to reset their brain's internal alarm clock. To do this, you'll need to gently wake up your child thirty to sixty minutes before their usual nighttime "alarm." You don't need to turn on the lights or play loud music, but you should rouse your child enough that you see their eyes flutter or have them roll over in bed. It may take a few nights for the body to unlearn its pattern. But with enough repetition, this should disrupt their sleep pattern and can help them leapfrog over that wired wake-up.

If you've attempted the dream pee and sleep reset, yet they continue to wake in the middle of the night, move on to the techniques found in the next section, "When They Don't Have to Go but Wake Up Anyway."

When They Don't Have to Go but Wake Up Anyway

Sometimes, your child may wake in the night and say they need to go potty, but when they sit . . . nothing happens. If this becomes a pattern, it's not that your child is trying to manipulate you, it's that they've discovered something powerful: when they say "I have to go potty," their parent comes running. At first, you can use the same techniques as we mentioned in the Stalling Tactics section above. But if this happens repeatedly without any actual elimination, you can safely start treating this as a night-waking issue, not a potty-training problem.

If you suspect your child is using potty requests as a new form of comfort-seeking, you're not alone—and you're not doing anything wrong. This is a totally normal twist in the nighttime parenting struggle, and it might be time to dust off some old parenting tools. If you've used sleep-training methods in the past—whether it's timed check-ins, gradual withdrawal, or another routine—it may be time to return to that familiar plan. You're not redoing potty training; you're reinforcing sleep skills your child already knows.

Nighttime Poops

Typically, children should stop pooping at night around eighteen months of age. However, when in the early phases of potty training, it's common for kids to begin pooping in their sleep diapers again.

At the very beginning, I wouldn't consider this a problem to solve. Give them a few weeks to adjust to their new rhythms and routines, and see if they naturally stop pooping at night.

If this pattern continues, it's time to put on your detective hat and figure out why. Are they withholding during the day because of fear of the potty? Do they want more privacy? Or is it just because they feel more relaxed in their bedroom environment? If you can identify the root cause, you can use the tactics found in other sections to address the issue.

If you think it's just that their biological rhythms have gotten out of whack, you may need to catch them in the act. If you can anticipate the timing of a nighttime poop, try to sit them on the potty before it happens to help them link up the sensation with the need to go.

Is This "Normal"?

As your potty-training journey continues, you may begin to wonder if your child is progressing at a "normal" pace. Despite knowing that comparison is the thief of joy, we all second guess ourselves at times and wonder if our kids are measuring up to their peers. If this is your first or only child, it's especially hard to know whether their skills and abilities (or lack thereof) are on track. You've heard enough of "every kid is different" and "they all learn at their own pace"—you want some hard data.

The problem is there's not a lot of consistent data to work from. Part of the problem, as we discussed earlier, is that it's difficult to identify exactly when you label a child as potty trained. Is your child fully trained after three days of no misses? What if they have a miss on the fourth day, are you back to square one? What if they need diapers on long car rides, but are okay at school? Are they "potty trained" yet? This is why *Good to Go* avoids using phrases like "ditch diapers for good," and instead emphasizes the continuum of parental involvement. It may be easier to estimate how long you'll be in the highly involved, occasionally involved, and rarely involved phases instead.

We took an informal poll of Laura's *Big Fat Positive* listeners and my former students, and gathered data on how long each phase lasted. In about 20 percent of the respondents, the highly involved phase lasted less than a week, and 25 percent said it lasted less than a month. However, the responses spanned a wide spectrum, with some respondents saying they were never highly involved, while others were still highly involved after more than a year.

You can see how difficult it is to find a benchmark for "normal." This is all complicated by the fact that many parents don't willingly share potty challenges, especially with older kids, because of shame and embarrassment.

Instead of worrying about your child's relative progress, I would challenge you to redefine what you think of as success. Think about what "potty independence" really means to you and your family. Maybe that means you want your child to be able to use public restrooms without a chaperone. Or it could mean that they tell you any time they need to go, but still need reassurance and company in the bathroom. Success could also be defined as having a child who is pooping daily in diapers to avoid constipation.

That said, potty training is an early opportunity to notice neurodivergent traits in children. As they navigate this new process, they may react intensely to the sensory experiences they encounter, like the texture of the toilet seats, the sound of flushing, or even the smells in a public restroom. In some children, these sensations can feel overwhelming, which can delay and complicate the potty-training process.

If you suspect your child may be neurodivergent, bring up your concerns with their pediatrician. They can refer you to specialists and therapists who can help you navigate a potential diagnosis. These practitioners have experience helping other families navigate potty training with neurodivergent kids and can give more specific and tailored advice.

When to Retire the Floor Potty

Parents are often eager to get rid of the small floor potties as soon as possible. And I get it, they can be unsightly and maybe even a little gross to have in your living room at all times. I would caution against rushing to ditch the floor potty too soon—doing so may increase misses and undermine your child's confidence.

Most children end up outgrowing the floor potty between ages three and four, but it can vary widely depending on the child. To gauge whether your child is ready, look for signs that they're ready to consistently use the regular toilet. This includes having enough lead time to reach the bathroom and physically navigating the higher toilet. You can test the first half of this by putting the floor potty in the bathroom.

Small children may still need parental help with setting up the big potty, like lifting the lid and making sure the seat insert is installed. If you have the ability to be there to help, you can feel more confident about removing the floor potty as an option. But, if you have other children to tend to or cannot physically assist your child, you may consider keeping the floor potty until your child is more confident on the big toilet, just to save your own sanity.

The day will come when you no longer have a potty in your living room, I promise! By following your child's cues and offering gentle encouragement, you will eventually be done with the floor potty for good.

A Potty Pause

There's one word I wish we could remove from our vocabulary around potty training: regressions. This word is casually bandied about by all kinds of so-called experts, but I believe it's inaccurate and harmful.

By this point, we all know that potty training is a learning process, not a binary state of existence. When you learn any new skill, there will be bumps in the road along the way. Think about learning a new skill as an adult. Maybe you've been practicing tennis for weeks and have developed a really solid backstroke. You have a match on Saturday, but on Friday, your boss threw you under the bus to cover his own mistake, and you can't stop ruminating on the injustice. During your tennis match, you can't hit a backstroke to save your life because you're distracted by personal problems. Just because you are distracted, hurt, or worried, it doesn't mean that you've somehow forgotten to play tennis or "regressed" in any way. You were just having a bad day.

With young toddlers, most learning has been fairly linear up to this point. Children have learned to pull up to a stand, cruise, then walk independently. If they wake up one day and can't walk anymore, this would be a true regression that should be brought up with a pediatrician. But potty training isn't linear, and sometimes forward progress takes a break or seems to backtrack a bit.

Sometimes, we must take a potty pause.

If you need to revisit using diapers, consider it more like having an off day on the tennis court. Your child isn't "regressing"—all the learning is still there, waiting to present itself when the conditions are right. Don't get dispirited or think there's something wrong with you or your child. Even if you're using diapers again, the groundwork you've laid with upskilling and modeling and narration is still being processed by your child. When it's time to try again, your child will likely progress faster than you expect.

So, how long should you pause? That's going to be different for every family. Since your child is still progressing and learning, this pause is as much for you as it is for your child.

A potty pause should last at least two weeks. This is enough time for everyone to regroup and shed the stress that led up to the pause. If you think the pause may last longer than a few weeks, I'd recommend putting away some of the potty props (books, floor potties, etc.) so their teaching impact isn't diluted. You want to protect the effectiveness of this gear and save it for when you restart the rehearsal period.

To determine if it's time to start again, first check in with yourself. Are you in an emotional and physical state to jump back into the highly involved phase? Then, check if your child has made more progress in the interim. Revisit the flowchart found in Chapter 3, "Rethinking Readiness," to see if your answers have changed. Maybe your child is showing more non-teachable signs, or they're responsive to some of the teachable components? On this second attempt, you'll want to stack things in your favor by having as many of these signs of readiness as possible.

If there's a big deadline coming up, like starting school, then you can use that as your new restart date and work backward two or three weeks.

And remember what we learned about asynchronous development in Chapter 3, "Rethinking Readiness"? Have you noticed that your child has accomplished a new milestone since you started the potty pause? Maybe they've learned how to jump with both feet, or started speaking in complex sentences. If this is the case, they may have been funneling their developmental energy into those skills, and now they're free to take on a new milestone.

Finally, use your intuition. There may not be a perfect checklist that works for your family, but you probably have a hunch about whether it's the right time. More than likely, all the effort you put into the first attempt will pay off this time around, and you will have a smoother experience the second time around.

AUGGIE'S LONG PAUSE

I mentioned this in the Introduction, so you already know that I considered Auggie's first attempt at potty training to be a total failure. After all, he spent about six months not using daytime diapers, only to start wearing them again for almost a full year.

Certainly, at the time, I thought this was a failure on my part. I thankfully didn't feel accusatory or disappointed in Auggie—I saved all that judgment for myself. I kicked myself for being so naive to think he was ready, and for jumping the gun. I thought, if only I had a time machine, I'd go back and do things differently.

But, when we started potty training him again just before he turned three, something interesting happened. Despite my trepidation about his willingness to learn (he seemed completely unmotivated and happy to stay in diaper forever), and my latent anxiety about my previous "failure," Auggie took to potty training almost instantly.

We had a little hiccup when it came to screen time, but after we took away that distraction, the child had zero misses. I couldn't believe it—this was the same child that had inspired so much potty-training stress the previous year!

At first, I attributed this near-instant success to two factors: his advanced age and Gia's help. And while both of those were definitely factors in his favor, Gia pointed out to me that Auggie hadn't been "regressing" all this time, after all. Instead, he had been continuing his learning, watching me and Corey use the potty and listening to our narration of our body cues, and storing away that knowledge for later.

Auggie didn't regress, he just took a really long pause.

Chapter in Review

- When considering a challenge, look for the root cause so you can tailor your approach.
- External motivation/rewards have their place, and can be effective if handled properly.
- Mild constipation can be managed at home with dietary changes, but more serious constipation needs the attention of your pediatrician.
- Beware of the pitfalls of comparison and keep in mind that potty training is not really "done" for quite some time.
- It's okay to take a break if needed. Consider this a potty pause, not a "regression."

10

Now We're Cruising

The Rarely Involved Phase

At some point in the not-too-distant future, you will realize that you have absolutely no idea when your kid last went to the bathroom. When you have an infant or toddler, this idea may seem impossible—up to now, you've been directly involved with every pee and poop since they were born. But this is the true end goal of "potty training"—one day, you will wipe their butt for the very last time.

But we're not quite there yet. By the time your kid turns six, they will, most likely, be on auto pilot with pottying. However, there's a lot of caveats, and there are certain scenarios where you will still need to provide assistance.

Public Bathrooms

Even if your child has the ability to be independent, there are occasions where you may not want them to go into public bathrooms by themselves. Not all public restrooms are safe for children, or perhaps the maintenance is lacking and you'd like to help them pick the cleanest stall.

This isn't much of a challenge if you and your child match genders. However, if you and your child have different gender identities, accompanying them in public bathrooms becomes increasingly difficult as they get older.

Obviously, if you can find an all-gender bathroom, or something labeled a "family bathroom," this is the best option. If you have another trusted adult who matches your child's gender, you may ask them to accompany them to the bathroom and wait outside the stall.

But if you don't have these options, approach the situation by centering your child's safety, rather than worrying about the comfort of strangers. This is easier for moms taking their sons into a women's restroom, as the common area is mostly for hand washing and all elimination is happening inside the stalls. Though you may get some strange looks, it's still considered socially acceptable and reasonable for moms to accompany their children into public restrooms.

The situation isn't as simple for dads who need to take their daughters into men's restrooms, where there may be men using urinals. This isn't as socially acceptable because there's less privacy in men's public bathrooms. If it's a small enough bathroom, the dad can peek in and see if the coast is clear, and ask other men to wait until your daughter is out of the bathroom.

If you're going somewhere where you know the bathrooms will be inaccessible, unsafe, or unsanitary, you may consider carrying a gender-inclusive disposable urinal bag with you. These fold down to a small packet, and can be kept in a pocket or purse. Sometimes, it's safer to find a protected corner, or shield your child with a jacket or blanket while they use the urinal bag, than it is to use the public restroom.

Continued Nighttime Involvement

As discussed in the previous section, many children need pull-ups or continue to wet the bed past age eight. This can present a social challenge for older children when they're invited to a sleepover. One option is to offer a "late-over" instead, and pick your child up that same night, even around ten o'clock or midnight. This is a popular choice among parents who have safety concerns about sleepovers, but still want to let their child attend the party. The benefit of this approach is that your child can save face and blame you for the early pickup!

If your child wants to stay but isn't comfortable wearing a pull-up under their pajamas, emphasize the importance of routine tries and encourage them to limit their fluid intake for a few hours before bed. This is also an opportunity to remind them that it's not the end of the world if they wet the bed, and that their friends and friends' parents will likely understand if it happens.

How and When to Remove Sleep Diapers

As previously discussed in Chapter 3, "Rethinking Readiness," nighttime dryness is not teachable—it's a complex developmental milestone that's dependent on physiological and neurological readiness. While other potty-training methods may give you techniques to force nighttime dryness, in my experience they're just not effective.

Most children don't start consistently waking up dry until they're between three and five years old, but many need pull-ups until ages eight or nine. This is why *Good to Go* doesn't claim that you'll "go diaper free" right away—most children will require sleep diapers for quite some time. You may also notice your child stays dry during naps, but not overnight. The main factor here is that naps are significantly shorter than nighttime sleep, so their bodies do not have to hold on to as much pee.

If your child continues to be wet at night, this is a normal and expected part of the process, and it doesn't reflect poorly on their daytime progress. Most children are daytime trained well before they are dry at night.

If you're trying to guess when your child will be ready, and they have relatives who are willing to dish the potty-training dirt, ask about when other members of the family were finally dry at night. You may find out that your uncle wasn't fully dry at night until he was in fourth grade, or that your child's birth parent was out of sleep diapers before daytime diapers. Take all this information with a grain of salt—there may be familial trends, but every child is different.

But at some point, even if it's years in the future, eventually you will need to remove sleep diapers. How do you know when it's time, and how do you do it?

A good rule of thumb is to remove sleep diapers once your child has woken up dry for five days in a row. This demonstrates that they have the bladder size and brain development to withhold their urine all night. I would also suggest that these be five "typical" days in your life—if all five days were while you're on vacation, wait until you get home and check to see if they're still dry in their normal environment.

You can tell your child, "You've been dry every morning this week! Tonight, we're going to try just wearing jammies and see what happens!" Instead of approaching nighttime dryness as "training," I'd take a curious approach to it and be flexible.

Prepare by setting up your child's bed for success. You'll want a good waterproof mattress protector (reusable or disposable both work) and a few extra sheets nearby. Many parents use "the lasagna method," where you create alternating layers of mattress protectors under sheets, three or four layers deep. This ingenious technique allows you to just strip off a soiled sheet without having to replace the whole setup in the middle of the night. (This is a valuable tool for future stomach flus, another common time when parents need to quick-change a bed.)

Many parents forget that the top sheet or blanket will often get wet as well, so having backup blankets (and, possibly, lovies or stuffed animals) are important. Set out some replacement jammies and wet wipes so you don't have to rummage through drawers at 2:00 a.m. If you bed share, you can use all the same approaches, but remember that your pajamas may also get wet, so plan accordingly.

If your child is still small enough for a floor potty, bring one into their bedroom for a short time. Just like during daytime training, their nighttime urgency awareness has a short lead time at first. If they do wake up and need to pee, there's more chance of success if there's a potty within eyesight. Also, many kids are scared to leave their room and navigate to a bathroom in the dark, so having a floor potty nearby will ease that fear.

If your child is still in a high-sided crib, you may consider switching them to a toddler bed so they can access the potty easier in the middle of the night. That said, I recognize that this is a huge transition in and of itself, so I would recommend doing the crib transition a few weeks before removing sleep diapers. Once they've settled in their new bed, you can remove nighttime diapers.

Though nighttime dryness can't be hurried, there are some things you can do to stack the cards in your favor. Reducing liquids in the evening and having them go commando in loose-fitting pajamas can both help.

SEBASTIAN FLIP-FLOPS

As I was gearing up to start potty training my younger son, Sebastian, I noticed something unexpected: he started waking up dry. Morning after morning, I would change him out of his pajamas and notice a completely dry diaper hiding underneath.

Of course, my anxious brain jumped straight to worrying that this was a sign of some kind of rare kidney disease. Thankfully, my mom (the pediatrician, ahem) reassured me that, as long as he was peeing enough during the day, he was probably just fine. "After all, do you pee while sleeping?" She asked me. "No, but I'm a grown up!" I responded.

During my next meeting with Gia, I brought up Sebastian's mysteriously dry mornings. This was all new to me because Auggie was such a notorious nighttime pee-er that we had to put additional absorbent pads in his pull-ups. (The child, to this day, drinks copious amounts of water, so it made sense.) I knew that the vast majority of children wear sleep diapers for years after daytime training, so I didn't know what to make of this development.

You've got a unicorn!" Gia exclaimed! She told me that it was very rare, but not-unheard-of for toddlers to develop nighttime dryness before they mastered daytime potty training.

> As I write this section, I realize this story may come off as a humblebrag, and I'm cringing at myself. But, the point of this story is not to celebrate his nighttime dryness, it's to highlight that I had absolutely nothing to do with it! I had the same level of control as everyone else—it's not like I could teach him this skill. Though it is absurdly funny to imagine secretly teaching my two-year-old to stay dry at night only, I really can't take credit.
>
> Hopefully this will help you realize, if your child is in sleep diapers longer than you had hoped, that there's nothing you did to cause it, and there's not much you can do to change it! They just have to get to that developmental milestone on their own, and we need to sit back and wait.

To Dream Pee or Not to Dream Pee?

Some parents are encouraged to sit their children on the potty a few hours after they go to sleep. The academic term for this is "lifting," probably because parents are physically picking up their sleeping children and placing them on a potty, hoping they'll empty their bladders and stay dry for the rest of the night. Some children don't wake up at all, hence the nickname "the dream pee"—this is similar to a "dream feed" you may remember doing with your infant.

Unfortunately, there's no evidence this has any benefit. In a number of clinical trials, lifting had no measurable benefit compared to placebo. Translation: dream pees don't work any better than just letting your kid sleep. In fact, some argue that lifting has a negative effect on nighttime dryness, because your children never get to experience the feeling of fullness and develop the skill of keeping it in.

Personally, I am more concerned with everyone getting a good night's sleep! If your child already wakes up in the middle of the night, you can absolutely use that time to take a quick trip to the potty.

But if your kid sleeps through the night, don't mess that up just for the illusion of nighttime dryness. If frequent bedwetting is waking everyone up and disrupting your sleep, then consider whether it's time to bring back pull-ups, or call your pediatrician to investigate a potential medical issue.

When to Call Your Doctor

Bedwetting is something you should feel comfortable bringing up to your child's pediatrician. They will be able to tell you if everything is normal, or whether there's a medical concern.

If your child is still in pull-ups at age seven, you should let their doctor know. While it's common for kids to still have issues with nighttime dryness up to age ten, it's best to let your pediatrician know about this issue a bit earlier. If they suspect a physiological issue, you can get the ball rolling on diagnosis and treatment before it becomes a bigger social issue for your child. (Sleepovers and summer camps are stressful occasions for kids with bedwetting concerns.)

If your kid has been dry at night for a few months and then suddenly starts wetting the bed, this could be a sign of a health problem like constipation, urinary tract infections, or diabetes. Your child may also have an issue that affects their ability to wake, like sleep apnea. If you notice any of the following symptoms, call your doctor right away:

- Pain during urination
- Excess thirst
- Pink or red urine
- Hard stools or constipation
- Losing weight
- Snoring

Re-Teaching the Basics

Even older kids will sometimes need to go back to basics. Even if it's met with an eye roll, you may need to continue reminding your child to attempt routine tries before movies, plane trips, and other activities.

If your child goes through a period of constipation, you may need to intervene and help them with a poop-friendly diet. Similarly, if your kid isn't drinking enough water, you should ask them to report on the color of their pee, and remind them that light yellow and clear is the goal, while dark yellow or cloudy is a warning sign. You can re-teach that their body is working hard to take care of them, and these things may be clues that they're not taking good care of their body.

When doing laundry, you may stumble across skid marks on their underwear. This is a sign that you may need to do some re-teaching around wiping, get some disposable wet wipes, or even invest in a bidet.

The goal is for them to create habits that are second nature. If you don't hear the sink running after a toilet flush, you may need to remind them to wash their hands.

This can also be the time when you teach about keeping the bathroom and toilet usable for the rest of the family. Show them how to wipe up stray pee drips on the seat, or how to use the toilet brush to remove any poop left on the inside of the bowl after flushing.

Now That We're "Done"

This has been quite a journey! I've walked you through every step of the potty-training process, from the early rehearsal period preparations to making sure your teenager flushes the toilet. Obviously, this is a lot of information to hold on to, and we've designed this book as a reference that you can revisit. During your potty-training process, you can flip back and forth between chapters as needed to refresh your memory and help you troubleshoot. But even more so, the hope is that the essential parenting tools found in this book will continue to be useful for years to come. As you move forward in parenting, remember that you've equipped your child with more than just the skill to use the toilet. You've developed problem-solving skills, taught emotional-regulation habits, and modeled persistence and confidence. These lessons will act as a foundation for other life lessons and transitions.

Now you can reflect and see what this process brought to light about you and your dynamic with your child. How did the process of teaching and learning a new skill feel for both of you? What did you notice about how your child approached learning that may be helpful for the future? What have you learned about yourself in the process? All these insights better equip you for what's to come in the wild ride of parenting, the joyful and the challenging, the highs and the lows, and the next big lessons ahead.

Chapter in Review

- Eventually, you will find yourself in the rarely involved phase and your child in the cruising phase. This is when you really are no longer intimately involved or even know about their potty habits.

- Removing sleep diapers will be based on how many mornings in a row your child wakes up dry. No need to "train" them during the night. Allow the body to do what it needs to do.

- Consult a physician if bedwetting continues past age seven, or if there is a change in potty habits or other health indicators.

- Learning lifelong bathroom habits takes time—focus on teaching how to care for their own bodies and leave bathrooms in a good state for others.

- The essential parenting tools found in *Good to Go* will serve you for years to come!

CONCLUSION

Hello, It's Laura Again!

In the introduction, I promised that I would tell you exactly how my younger son's potty-training journey turned out. When Gia and I started writing this book, Sebastian was still in diapers. Is it possible this book idea was all just a plot for me to get free private coaching from Gia? *I'll never tell.*

Whether my methods were ethical or not, I had the significant advantage of having a twenty-year veteran parenting coach at my side throughout potty training. I also had the benefit of all the time I had spent researching and refining the *Good to Go* method alongside Gia, so I was becoming a bit of an expert myself.

This is going to be easy, I thought. I've got this.

Sigh.

Look, even with the best professional help, potty training can be a humbling experience. All my hubris about the process crumbled quickly when faced with the reality of my precious, hilarious, and independent AF toddler.

We started the rehearsal period at the beginning of December, when he was two months shy of turning three (that's thirty-four months for you data nerds). I was hesitant to start much sooner because of my previous "failure" with Auggie and hoped that waiting until he was older would yield better results.

My version of the rehearsal period relied heavily on modeling and narration, offering up the potty (we already had floor potties around for Auggie, who still used them occasionally), and giving him some post-bath naked time. Honestly, the practice naked time was mostly a result of my husband, Corey, and I being too tired to catch him, but he managed to stay dry during those sessions, so I was hopeful. We also did a few upskills, like changing diapers in the bathroom, practicing undressing, and washing our hands after every diaper change.

We talked about taking away his daytime diapers for about a week before we actually did it and really hyped up the difference between daytime and nighttime diapers. (His nighttime diapers had Elmo and Cookie Monster on them, while his waking diapers were boring and white.) It seemed like he was getting on board, and he'd say things like "no more diapers, only underwear!"

We planned the rehearsal period to lead into his winter holiday break, hoping to utilize the two weeks he had off school to master potty training. After all, we weren't traveling and had no houseguests—it seemed like a great time to start.

December 23 was our first day of official potty training. You know, *two days before Christmas*. This is where we made our first mistake. In retrospect, trying to introduce potty training during the holiday season was optimistic at best.

I mean, at first it seemed fine. Sebastian woke up psyched to put on his brand-new Blippi undies and even had a pee in the potty first thing! All morning he did great and peed once more before naptime. But things unraveled in the afternoon. While I was busy making pies for Christmas dinner, Corey walked into the playroom to discover Sebastian independently playing in the corner . . . with soaking wet pants.

The next few days followed this trajectory, with all of us being distracted by holiday preparations, and Sebastian soiling himself without skipping a beat in his play.

I'm not sure exactly what happened on each day, because like the captain's log during a typhoon, all I have left in my notes is "December 27th: abandoning ship."

Even newly minted experts need to take a potty pause, guys.

My notes pick back up in February, where I write "postponing for the third time: too many birthday parties, swim classes and field trips!" Ah, to be a toddler with a full social calendar, what a life.

Finally, in early March, we decided to try again. Instead of trying to find an elusive weekend with no activities, we just canceled all plans and blocked off our calendar. By this point, Sebastian had turned three, and we were ready to get this show on the road.

Unlike the two weeks we gave ourselves the first time, we didn't even pick a three-day weekend for this attempt. We had realized that our last attempt was just poorly timed—we were all way too distracted and taken out of our normal routines. This time, we were going all in, and I knew Sebastian would benefit from all the learning he had already done. I knew we weren't starting from scratch this time.

On day one, Corey and I divided and conquered. In the morning, I stayed home with Sebastian while Corey took Auggie out on a fun daddy-son adventure. Then we swapped. I also made sure to hide my phone so I wasn't distracted.

I'll save you the play-by-play narrative, here's the stats:

- Day 1: 3 pee misses
- Day 2: 1 pee miss when both parents were busy with Auggie
- Day 3: Back to school, only 1 pee miss
- Day 4: No misses at school or at home!
- Day 5: Said his tummy hurts on the drive home—a poo cue! Pulled over to find small poop in undies, but he finished in the travel potty!

It's been over six months now since we potty trained, and after that first week, misses have been few and far between. He's made amazing progress, and we've gotten to the point where I don't feel anxious about long outings or car rides. We've even taken a plane trip and successfully navigated scary airport bathrooms.

The other day, I realized that neither of my children had used the floor potty in a long while. As I picked it up to take it to the basement, I was surprised to feel a wave of sadness and nostalgia wash over me. I realized that my boys, who I could swear had just been tiny babies a few moments ago, were now turning into big kids. I found myself crying over the floor potty, unwilling to move it from its symbolic spot in our living room.

That's when Sebastian wiggle-danced into the room, pulled down his pants, and peed in the floor potty. He looked up at me from his low perch and asked, "mama, why you crying?" I laughed and said, "no reason, my baby." Wiping away my tears, I got back to parenting: "Was that a poop or a pee?"

And with that, Sebastian saved me from retiring the floor potty for now. I know I'll have to get rid of it eventually, but we'll do it when we're all ready.

Gia and I want to thank you for taking the time to read *Good to Go*. We know parenting is hard work, and we are touched that you've chosen to spend your precious free time learning the methods in this book.

RESOURCES

For a regularly updated list of children's books, products, songs, and other media that will help you in your potty-training journey, including direct links, visit https://goodtogoparenting.com/resources/.

For more support, to find our social media, and to get updates on all the *Good to Go* happenings, visit https://goodtogoparenting.com.

ACKNOWLEDGMENTS

We want to thank The Family Room and its founder, Karen Stoteraux, for bringing us together. Without the space she created for families to be supported, Laura and I would never have met. It was in these parenting groups that we began to see a vision for *Good to Go*.

Having an idea to write a book is one thing, finding an agent that whole-heartedly believes in your vision and sees potential beyond what we could imagine is another. It is a fact that this book would not exist without the support of our agent, Amanda Bernardi! Thank you to Christen Karniski of Rowman & Littlefield for her belief in our vision and bringing this book into the world.

While many families have already benefited from the *Good to Go* potty-training method, there were some early adopters who shared their stories with us, which helped shape the trajectory of this book. Grace Bergland shared meticulous notes of her journey which sparked many interesting conversations and ideas that made their way into these pages. Karina Vesco, long-time friend of Gia's, shared her unique perspective that helped shape many of the aspects of this book. Bret Vandenbos, a parent and writer, got one of the earliest copies of *Good to Go* and helped steer us in the right direction. A huge thanks to an early supporter, Danielle Takata-Herring of Dreambox, who created the first upskills image and brought this concept to life.

Gia's Acknowledgments

When I first reached out to Laura about writing this book, I was so nervous. Sharing parenting tips in class was one thing, but asking her to write a book together felt like a huge leap. The words barely left my mouth and she was all in! I could not have asked for a better writing partner. To say this book would not have happened without her is an understatement! There are so many other people to thank but first and foremost are my two children, Gian Martin and Marcus. They encouraged me every step of the way and were the original inspiration for *Good to Go*. To my sister, Jenna Gambaro, for her absolute belief in me and ongoing source of strength. To my mother, Susan LaPittus, my number one cheerleader, who unwaveringly believed in my ability to pull this off. To Sherry Sirotnik, for her willingness to hear snippets of the book in its beginning stages and always providing enthusiastic feedback. A personal thanks to my bestie, Karina Vesco, for her insights and support.

Laura's Acknowledgments

When Gia approached me to write this book, I couldn't say yes fast enough! I like to joke that this book was just a long con to have her as my own personal parenting coach. The truth is that Gia's generosity, humor, and insight is totally unmatched, and I couldn't have asked for a better co-author.

This book would not have been possible without the support of my husband, Corey Evett, a brilliant writer himself, who took on extra childcare and household duties so I could work long hours to get *Good to Go* out in the world. Thank you, my love. And thank you to my mom, Dr. Susan Winter, for fielding medical questions, reminding me of embarrassing stories from my own potty-training experience, and loving me unconditionally. I would also like to thank my stepfather Dr. Neil Buist, my mother-in-law Sheri Snyder, and my brother Jeff Birek for always being supportive and wonderful.

Thank you to my BFF and *Big Fat Positive* podcast co-host, Shanna Yager, for being so supportive of this project! And thank you to Jessie Glenn, Alissa Rowinsky Wright, and Jessica Luther for providing research and insights during the writing process.

I'd also like to thank everyone who provided childcare for my young sons during this time, especially their teachers Ms. Flores,

Ceci, Lyndsi, Uma, Vivi, and Wendy. Knowing my children were safe and well-cared for is a joy and a privilege, and without this support I know I wouldn't have enough time or energy to put my work out into the world.

Finally, thank you to my children, "Auggie" and "Sebastian," who not only taught me many lessons on potty training, but also how to love fully and deeply, even while making fart jokes. You two are the lights of my life.

INDEX

accidents/misses   2, 55, 88, 120, 121, 125, 145, 151, 153, 166, 167, 175, 182, 199
action awareness   119
air travel   148–51
already-potty-trained classmates   145
asynchronous development   40, 41

bedtime delays and overnight challenges
   middle-of-the-night wakings   178
   like clockwork at same time every night   179
   really needing to pee   178
   waking up even without needing to go   180
   nighttime poops   180–1
   stalling tactics   176–7
bedwetting   43, 193
body awareness   42, 68, 166, 177, 179
   types of   119
      action awareness   119
      sensation awareness   119
      urgency awareness   120
boredom activities   116–17
boxers/briefs   105–6
BRAT diet   174

capitulation   28
caregivers   9, 10, 12, 55, 56, 167
children's potty book   101–3

cloth diapers   12
clothes   88–9, 96, 150
cognitive signs of readiness   37, 38
compromise   28–30, 127, 146, 169
consistent vocabulary   11, 54
constipation   55, 182, 194
   anti-constipation foods   174
   chronic constipation   172, 173
co-parenting   55, 56
coping skills   31, 50
core values   16, 66, 165
cozy corner   31
criticisms   59

daytime diapers   87, 88, 119, 130, 185, 190, 198
decision-making flowchart   44
defiant behavior   169–70
descriptive praise   24–6, 165
developmental focus   40
developmental milestones   12, 14, 35, 40, 189, 192
diarrhea   172, 173
discipline   26, 168
disposable diapers   12
distraction   107, 141, 149, 167, 176
dream pee   178, 179, 192

easy-to-remove clothing   130
emotional co-regulation   122
emotional hygiene routine   31, 112
   intangible tools   32
   tangible tools   32

emotional regulation   31, 32, 38, 39, 112
encopresis   153, 173
evaluative praise   24, 25
The Explosive Child (Greene)   169
extra-absorbent underwear   105

fears   8, 163–4, 174, 191
first-time parents   7, 22
floor potties   70, 90, 93, 95–7, 120, 149, 200
   comfort   91
   novelty features   91
   retiring   182–3
   seat height   90–1
   splash guard   91
   transition features   91

gastrocolic reflex   173
gear categories   90
   floor potties   90–1
   potty accessories   93–4
   toilet seat attachments   92–3
genitals   10
grandparents   58–9

high-conflict parenting dynamic   56
high-involvement phase   51, 53, 63, 65, 122, 128, 129, 141, 146, 176, 181

illogical consequences   27, 171
indifference   170–1
intangible tools   32
interoception   42

jealousy   106

lactose intolerance   174
lasagna method   190
late-over   188

learning process   14, 41, 55, 64, 65, 84, 93, 96, 104, 112, 120, 122, 125, 128, 138, 139, 142, 148, 183, 184, 195, 199
lifting   192
logical consequence   26, 27, 170, 171

medical issues   54
middle-of-the-night wakings   178
   like clockwork at same time every night   179
   really needing to pee   178
   waking up even without needing to go   180
mild constipation   173
miss kit   146, 147, 150, 155, 156
modeling   72–4, 84, 107, 165

naps/naptime   36, 108, 130, 133, 134, 143, 145, 189, 198
narration   72–4, 197
natural consequences   26, 170
negotiation sequence   27, 126
   sealing deal   30–1, 127–8
   sharing perspectives   29, 127
   teaching compromise   29–30, 127
nighttime diapers   87, 177, 191
nighttime dryness   43, 87, 189–93
nighttime involvement   188–9
nighttime poops   180–1
night training   43
non-flushable wipes   94
non-teachable signs   54, 184
non-teachable skills   36, 79

occasionally involved phase   141, 150
oppositional defiant disorder (ODD)   169
overactive bladder   124

parcopresis   174
parental authority   28
parental intervention   15, 26
parental involvement   64, 122, 181
   stages   53
      potty training   122
      teaching *versus* learning   14
parenting   2, 7, 10, 13, 16, 20, 55, 195
   challenges   72, 176
   generational differences   58
   resources   3, 52
   tools   9, 46, 180, 195
pee   42, 84, 124, 126
   accidents/misses   2
   emergencies   95
   sitting
      advantages   113
      disadvantages   113
   standing up
      advantages   114
      disadvantages   114
   surprise   152
peer-to-peer teaching   145
perfectionism   165
performance anxiety   164–5
"P" foods   173
phimosis   114–15
physical signs   36, 37
plane bathrooms   148
play-based learning   97
   play-based instruction   99–100
   pretend play   98–9
   reading books   100–1
poop-friendly diet   194
posture   76–9, 85
potty accessories   93
   books and toys   94
   dressing chair   94
   full change of clothes   94
   non-flushable wet wipes   93–4

small trash can with lid   94
step stools   93
potty awareness   42
potty dance   51, 126, 145, 166
potty pause   176, 183–5
potty persuasion   151, 153
   aiming games   152
   not-quite five senses   152–3
   "prove me wrong"   151–2
   race/fly to the potty   152
   surprise pee   152
potty preview   147–9, 155, 156
potty signs   122–3
potty struggles   2
power struggles   28, 31, 72, 75, 174
pregnancy/adoption   54
preschools   8, 57, 80, 88, 96, 148
pressure pitfalls   153
props
   filling up balloon   99–100
   raisins in the pot!   100
public bathrooms   95, 163, 187–8
pull-ups   52, 138, 147, 150, 172, 188, 189, 193

readiness   35, 41, 50, 63, 150, 184
   cognitive   38, 51
   flow chart   45
   physical   37
   signs of   37, 38, 109, 110, 184
   social-emotional   38–9
reading books   100–1
regression   143, 183
rehearsal period   9, 63–5, 68, 72, 76, 77, 79, 87, 96, 97, 103, 106, 109, 138, 145, 170, 184, 194, 197, 198
   modeling and narration   73–4
resistance   125–6, 169–70
re-teaching basics   194
rewards   171, 175

routine tries   55, 74–6, 85, 106, 131, 133–7, 149, 154, 156, 157, 167, 173, 176, 189, 194

sample schedules
   advanced schedule   153–60
   day one   130–8
scaffolding   21, 83
school   83, 138, 185
   deadline   109
   diapers   88, 145
   return to   143–5
screen time   25, 97, 103, 115, 128, 167–9, 186
sensation awareness   54, 119
   lack of   175–6
shy bowel   174
siblings   106, 167
   older sibling   106–7
   tandem training   110–11
   twins and other multiples   109–10
   younger sibling   109
singing songs   103
sleep   126, 176, 179, 192, 193
   apnea   193
   diapers   102, 130, 178
      removal   189–91
   pattern   179
   skills   180
sleepovers   188, 189
social-emotional signs   36–9
sole-parents   56
squatting position   37, 77, 78, 173
stalling tactics   176–7, 180
standing to pee   113, 114, 152
step stool   77, 91–3, 95
subtractive reinforcement   171, 175

tangible tools   32
tantrums   112

toilet paper   80–3, 106
toilet seat attachments   92
   permanent seat attachments   92
   removable inserts   92
   step-stool inserts   92–3
travel gear   94–5
travel potties   95, 138, 146, 148
travel urinal   95

underwear   52, 104, 105, 147, 194
Universal Potty Sequence (UPS)   38, 66–8, 79, 96, 99, 107, 119, 138, 147, 175
upskilling   20, 21, 68, 73, 79, 89, 103, 109, 119, 184, 198
   car-seat conundrums   23–4
   mealtimes   22
   the UPS   68–72
urgency awareness   120, 190
   lead time   124
urine stream   115

Values-Centered Parenting (VCP) tool   12, 15, 165
   avoiding trips to urgent care   17–19
   body aware   66
   kindness   19
   for poop and pee   65–6
   usage   16–17
Vygotsky, Lev   21

wiping   37, 79, 144, 194
   find position   82–3
   scrunch/fold   80
   washing hands   83
   without wiping   83
withholding   78, 153, 173, 180

Zone of Proximal Development (ZPD)   21

ABOUT THE AUTHORS

Gia Gambaro Blount is a child development and parent education instructor, guest speaker, and parenting consultant with over twenty years of experience. Gia has an M.A. in Early Childhood Development, a B.A. in Developmental Psychology, and is a mother of two children so different from one another they have challenged her understanding of parenting theories and deepened her awareness that there is no "right" way to parent. Gia's contributions include founding the Pasadena City College Family Resource Center, serving as a board member for the North East Los Angeles Forest Schools, teaching a UCLA xOpen series, and presenting at numerous conferences and schools. Gia co-authored the current California Department of Education Parent Education curriculum for Pasadena City College. She has been featured in HuffPost, AARP Family & Relationships, and Shout Out LA. She is the Toddler Expert for The Family Room, has been interviewed as an expert on several top parenting podcasts, and is a scouted keynote speaker for preschools, family centers, and corporations.

Laura Birek is a writer, podcaster, storyteller, and mom to two young boys. She is the author of *Picture Perfect Knits* (Chronicle, 2006) and has written for *Parents Magazine*; *O, The Oprah Magazine*; *The Los Angeles Times*; *Shondaland*; *xoJane*, and more. Since 2018, Laura has been co-hosting the weekly podcast *Big Fat Positive*, named one of the best pregnancy and parenting podcasts by *Refinery29*, *Verywell Family*, and *Giggle Magazine*. With over three-and-a-half million downloads and counting, *Big Fat Positive* has established Laura as a trusted and influential resource for parents around the world.